MONSTER PARTIES AND GAMES

MONSTER
PARTIES AND GAMES
Fifteen Film-Based Activities

CHRIS KULLSTROEM

McFarland & Company, Inc., Publishers
Jefferson, North Carolina, and London

ALSO BY CHRIS KULLSTROEM

Making a Monstrous Halloween:
Themed Parties, Activities and Events (McFarland, 2009)

Illustrations by Karli Hendrickson.
Images in Chapter 13 are used with permission from the
Fred D. Phening, III, collection.

LIBRARY OF CONGRESS CATALOGUING-IN-PUBLICATION DATA

Kullstroem, Chris, 1979–
Monster parties and games : fifteen film-based activities /
Chris Kullstroem.
p.   cm.
Includes bibliographical references and index.

ISBN 978-0-7864-4371-0
softcover : 50# alkaline paper ∞

1. Parties — Planning.   2. Fantasy games — Planning.   3. Monster
films — Social aspects.   I. Title.
GV1471.K63   2009   793.2 — dc22   2009013752

British Library cataloguing data are available

Cover illustration by Karli Hendrickson; background ©2009 Shutterstock

Manufactured in the United States of America

McFarland & Company, Inc., Publishers
Box 611, Jefferson, North Carolina 28640
www.mcfarlandpub.com

TO ALL THE HORROR, SCI-FI AND
MONSTER BUFFS OUT THERE.
ROCK ON.

ACKNOWLEDGMENTS

Special thanks to Donnie Owens, a true supporter of the arts. Also thanks to Anders Kullstroem, who may be playing games in his sleep by now. Additional thanks to fellow game players and supporters: James Carson, Tim Carson, Mollie Clarke, Jonathan M. and Michael J. Covault, Dean Davis of Monster Guts, Scott Ferman, Sean and Tammi Flynn, Rick Gipstein, Matt Greene, Judy Griffin, Circus Historical Society, Kevin Keegan, Therese Kus, Jacob Larimore, Debbie Mcguy and Don Staub, Cathy Packer, Fred D. Pfening, III, Lori Schenking, Jaimie Sixsmith, Dave Szankovics, Theresa Valli, Jim and Kathy Walsh, Sharon Waxmundsky, Lawrence M. Zaccaro.

TABLE OF CONTENTS

INTRODUCTION

An invincible race of aliens invades your home town. Blood-thirsty werewolves charge through the woods. Hordes of zombies break through the windows. Demons are conjured to steal your soul. We see them in the theater and watch the marathons at home, eyes glued to the screen at midnight and a world away from our living room. And from the opening scenes to the closing credits, we become the victims, the heroes, and even the monsters themselves: running for our lives, battling the creature or stalking our prey before the final kill. We lose ourselves and enter the world of our darkest nightmares, where anything could happen and our very lives may lay on the line.

But after the movies come to their happy or gruesome ends, are the battles really over? Are the moments of the chase and ruthless slaughter truly confined to the screen, and our only gateway into them through the magic of the remote control? We've survived the invasions, the awakenings, the conjurings and the mutilations — if only there was a way to continue the adventures back in our own world.

But there is! You may have entered the nightmares of so many others, but now you can enter your own to see just what could happen and who will survive. With *Monster Parties and Games*, you have a collection of themed games that you can make yourself to bring to life your favorite films in the horror, science fiction and dark comedy genres. These games can be played by all ages and range from zombie card games to murder mysteries. Long after the stories on the screen have ended, yours will just begin as you run, fight, dance, bleed, raise the dead and try to come out alive in each and every one.

Favorite Flicks

Each game is themed after a specific monster film, ranging from classics of the 1940s to those of modern day. Each includes shocks, scares, laughs and suspense, making them some of the best of their genre.

You may find that it makes the games more fun to watch the accompanying film either before or after you play. Combining the two can make the games seem much more true to life and produce a closer connection to the films. Together, they make a fun and freaky game and movie night for you and your friends and family. One game, *Run for your Life!*, is actually played *while* watching the film.

1

Game Creations

Some of the games allow players to use their imaginations and be creative, while others focus on problem solving and deduction. Some deal with keeping journals of deadly activities while others involve dancing and digging up graves. Sometimes players work together. Other times they try and kill each other. But in each case, players are put in situations similar to the characters in the films. Most can be played over and over again, and each chapter gives examples on how you can make them unique with your own personal madness.

Supplies and Props

Some games require no more than photocopying a few pages from the book and taping them onto blank index cards, while others require a variety of supplies and props. For a quick glance at which games require what supplies, check out the *Game Pieces* chart on pages (5 and 6). This chart lists items used for making multiple games in the book. However, additional items may be needed, all of which are listed at the beginning of each chapter. Some props that you may not currently own, such as skeleton bones and body parts, are used as décor or even clues in the games. These can be found at Halloween shops and craft shops around October, or purchased online throughout the year. You'll find that using these death props brings a whole new dimension to games: horrific atmospheres in which deadly creatures, serial killers and other monsters can truly come to life.

Game Sheets

Depending on the type of game or party being played, each chapter also includes an *Object of the Game* page, *Host Sheet* or both. These pages are meant to be photocopied and used as an easy reference to rules so that you won't need to flip through the book to keep things straight. However, it's always best to re-read the chapter before playing the game so that you won't be too dependent on these pages.

Choosing the Monster Nights

Some of the larger party games in this book may inspire you to put them together around Halloween or for a truly twisted birthday party, while card and board games can add the perfect touch to a Friday night horror film fest. In all, they can help you and your friends bring out your inner monsters for some grisly, murderous fun any time of year.

The Monster Disclaimer

To make these games true to the nature of the films, many deal with subjects of myth, magic, devils and spiritual belief. But fear not: each game is for entertainment purposes only, and is not meant to be used for the sake of evil intent, demon conjuring or human sacrifice — unless you *really* want them to be.

GAME PIECES CHART

	1. The Curse of the Wolf	2. You're Next!	3. Order of the True Believer	4. The Wrong Experiment	5. The Nightly Haunt	6. Ghostbusters: On the Case	7. Mr. Grave's Gathering	8. The Addams Clan Party	9. Witches and Warlocks	10. Freddy's Dream House	11. Dolls from Hell	12. Where the Dead Walk	13. Run for your Life!	14. Hell and Damnation	15. Surrounded
Bones/Skull					×			×							
Colored Gem Stones									×						
Costumes								×							
Craft Die						×									
Egg Timer				×						×					
Index Cards	×	×		×			×	×		×	×				×
Fake Blood					×		×			×	×				
Fake Body Parts					×			×		×					
Fake Dummy					×		×			×					
Fake Weapons					×		×			×	×				
Gift Bags					×		×	×							
Gold Coins								×	×					×	
Prizes					×		×	×		×			×		
Poster Board									×			×	×		
Regular Die		×							×						
Rope					×		×	×		×					
Scrapbook/Sketch Book			×								×				
Small Stones									×			×		×	
Tools							×	×							
Tombstones								×							
Vials					×		×		×						

SECTION 1

CLASSIC HORROR AND SCIENCE FICTION THRILLERS

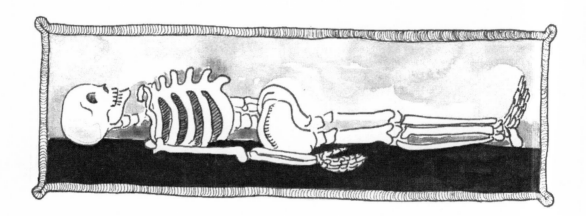

Horror and science fiction films of the 1940s and 1950s set the groundwork for the genre as we know it today. Werewolves, vampires and ghosts made some of their first appearances on the silver screen and The Cold War and creation of the atom bomb influenced monster tales of world invasion, scientific breakthroughs and the future of mankind as we know it. Together, they gave the world a new form of nightly entertainment and the first generation of movie-goer monster fanatics was born.

Watching the classics, we are brought back to a time when the element of shock value was new and anticipation was high. Suspense was a major factor in these films and even today we find ourselves gripping our seats and holding our breath as the killer moves in on his victim in the final scenes.

The films in this section were chosen from many classics for their great storylines, demented characters and haunting atmospheres that will make you want to step right into the screen and get into all the action. The games they inspired will allow you to do just that, as you run from the Wolf Man or become a werewolf yourself, fight or succumb to the Pod People from another world and study the occult while avoiding an ancient demon. You'll also find yourself deformed after a horrific experiment gone terribly wrong and step into a murder mystery in which anyone could end up dead.

Many horror and science fiction films take real world scenarios and add a daunting twist, asking that universal question, "What if...?" Whether you grew up with these classic tales or you're encountering them for the first time, you may find that the answer to that question is a lot more sinister than you thought.

1

THE CURSE OF THE WOLF

Werewolf Card Game
based on *The Wolf Man (1941)*,
4–6 players

The Wolf Man is a monster movie that heavily influenced future generations of were-wolf films. Yet unlike modern adaptations that primarily focus on bodily mutations and people getting ripped to shreds, this early tale centers on a man's inner struggle with the knowledge that he has become a killer against his will, as he seeks help from those around him to keep his loved ones out of mortal danger. The scene of Lon Chaney, Jr.'s werewolf transformation was revolutionary in its time, and though it does not involve the high-tech special effects we have come to expect today, it will always be viewed as a classic horror movie moment.

THE GAME

In this card game, the curse of the wolf has already clawed its way into some of the players, and it is slowly revealed over time just who is affected. Both humans and were-wolves must be mindful of every play, as each may lead to the ultimate victory of killing off the others so that theirs is the only kind left alive. You will need:

- 29 4 × 6" Plain Index Cards • Double-Sided Tape • Scissors

PREPARING THE GAME

To make *The Curse of the Wolf*, you'll need to put together 2 sets of cards: Character Cards and Playing Cards.

CHARACTER CARDS assign players as Humans or Werewolves at the start of the game. Photocopy the Character cards below and tape each onto a 4 × 6" plain index card **cut in half lengthwise**. You'll need a total of 3 Human cards and 3 Werewolf cards.

The **PLAYING CARDS** are very similar to an ordinary deck of cards with 4 suits of 13 cards. Suits consist of Wolf, Pentagram, Blood and Moon and each bear their own symbol. Certain cards can be used to kill off Humans, and others can be used to kill Werewolves. To make the deck, photocopy the Aces, face cards and numbered cards below and tape onto 4 × 6" plain index cards **cut in half lengthwise**. The face cards of the main deck contain images from the film: Silver Cane (King), the Gypsy (Queen) and the Wolf Man (Jack). You'll need one 1 of the Ace cards and **4 copies** of the face cards so that you have one for each suit. When making the face cards, draw the symbol of each suit in the upper right hand corner of the card, with the following exceptions:

- The Silver Cane of the **Wolf suit** does not contain claw marks, but has Wolf written under the number 10.
- The Gypsy of the **Wolf suit** does not contain claw marks, but has Wolf written under the number 10.
- **All Wolf Man cards** contain claw marks, **in addition** to their suit symbol.

Finally, make 9 copies of the numbered cards (2–10), and write their numbers in the center of the cards.

PLAYING THE GAME

The game begins by dealing each player a Character card to assign them as a Human or Werewolf. Players should look at their Character cards and then keep them **face down** throughout the game. The number of Humans and Werewolves will depend on the number of players:

- *4 players:* 2 Werewolves, 2 Humans
- *5 players:* 2 Werewolves, 3 Humans
- *6 players:* 3 Werewolves, 3 Humans

Players are then dealt 4 playing cards. Each turn, a player picks up **1 card** from the deck and discards 1 card to a face-up discard pile. The next player (clockwise from the dealer) must then either match the suit *or* the number of the discarded card. If they cannot, they must pick up the **entire** discard pile. The object of the game for Humans is to kill all the Werewolves. The object for Werewolves is to kill all Humans. However, since Character cards are kept face down, it will only be revealed over time just who is who.

GETTING KILLED. Werewolves are killed by having 2 Silver Cane cards in their hand at once. Humans are killed when they have 28 or more claw marks in their hand at once. This is determined by players adding up the number of claw marks in their hand each turn. (For example: A Wolf Ace [13 points] and a Wolf 10 [10 points] equals 23 claw marks.) Therefore, players should try to get rid of their highest claw mark cards whenever possible. Humans will do this to stay alive and Werewolves will do this to kill off Humans. At the start of each turn, drawing a claw card or Silver Cane card **does not** immediately kill a player. As long as they have less than 2 Silver Cane cards or 28 claw marks after they discard, they are not killed. It is only at the **end** of a player's turn that they are killed if they have the required cards. On the first round of play, players cannot be killed by the original cards they are dealt. They may put down 2 cards on their first turn if they have to in order to save their lives. When a player is killed, they reveal their Character card to the group and their cards are shuffled back into the draw pile.

ADDITIONAL PLAYS. Playing the Ace of Pentagrams gives the player the option to get rid of as many cards as they wish to the **bottom** of the draw pile. Once the draw pile has been gone through and only the discard pile remains, players do not pick up a card with each turn, but only **discard** a card each turn. If a player runs out of cards and is unable to discard, they must pick up the entire discard pile.

WINNING THE GAME. The game continues until all the Humans are killed or all the Werewolves are killed.

MAKE THIS GAME YOUR OWN!

Make your version of The Curse of the Wolf *original by drawing your own pictures for the Ace cards and face cards, as well as strange, scary or goofy pictures for the Character cards.*

The Curse of the Wolf

Object of the Game

Humans: Kill off all Werewolves
Werewolves: Kill off all Humans
Killing a Human: 28 or more claw marks
Killing a Werewolf: 2 Silver Canes

Players are each dealt a Character card and 4 playing cards. Remaining playing cards are put face down as the main deck. Players look at their Character cards and then keep them face down in front of them.

EACH TURN. Each turn, a player picks up **1 card** from the main deck and discards 1 card to a face up discard pile. When discarding, players must match either the suit or the number of the previous discarded card. If they cannot, they must pick up the **entire** discard pile.

GETTING KILLED. Werewolves are killed by having 2 Silver Cane cards in their hand at once. Humans are killed when they have 28 or more claw marks in their hand at once. *(For example: A Wolf Ace [13 points] and a Wolf 10 [10 points] equals 23 claw marks.)* Therefore, players should try to get rid of their highest claw mark cards whenever possible.

Cards do not kill off players until the **end** of their turn. As long as a player has less than 2 Silver Cane cards or 28 claw marks after they discard, they are safe. *On the first round of play, players cannot be killed by the original cards they are dealt. They may put down 2 cards on their first turn if they have to in order to save their lives.* When a player is killed, they reveal their Character card to the group and their cards are shuffled back into the draw pile.

ADDITIONAL PLAYS. Playing the Ace of Pentagrams gives players the option to place **as many cards as they wish** from their hand to the bottom of the draw pile.

Once the draw pile is gone and only the discard pile remains, players do not pick up a card each turn but only **discard** a card each turn. If a player runs out of cards or is unable to discard, they must pick up the entire discard pile.

WINNING THE GAME. The game continues until all the Humans are killed or all the Werewolves are killed.

Character Cards

Character Card:
WOLF MAN

Character Card:
HUMAN

Character Card:
WOLF MAN

Character Card:
HUMAN

Aces

ACE 13	ACE 13
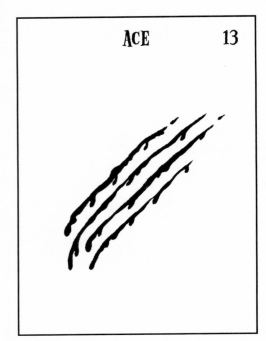	
ACE 13	ACE 13

	DISCARD CARDS

Face Cards

SILVER CANE   10

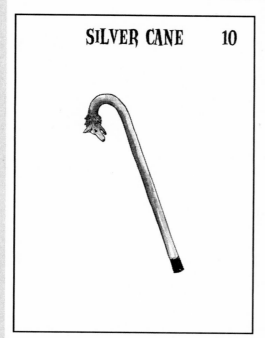

GYPSY   10

THE WOLF MAN   10

Numbered Cards

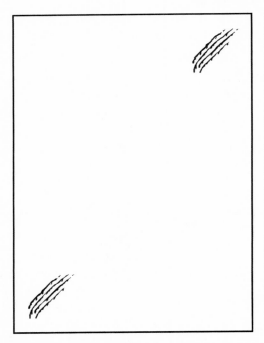

COPY @ 120%

2
YOU'RE NEXT!

Mutation Card Game
based on *Invasion of the Body Snatchers (1956),*
5–8 players

Invasion of the Body Snatchers is a psychological thriller that came out in a time when communism paranoia abounded. Based on Jack Finney's novel, the human race becomes threatened in a world-wide takeover by beings out to destroy all that makes man what he is. And with no match against the strength of the enemy, the question remains: would you succumb, or would you fight?

The film is as shocking to watch today as it was back in its release in 1956, effectively producing the feeling of utter helplessness as the invasion spreads far and fast, with our demise inevitable and no one left to trust.

THE GAME

In this mutation card game, each play could be your last ... as a human. Players take on roles of either humans running from pod people or pod people trying to turn humans into their own kind. At the start of the game, no one knows who is who, but with each turn it is slowly revealed just who can be trusted and who should be destroyed. You will need:

- 38 4 × 6" Plain Index Cards • Pencil **for each Player** • Regular Die
- Scissors • Double-Sided Tape • Optional Supplies: Printer Labels

PREPARING THE GAME

To make *You're Next!*, you'll need to create the following: Character Cards, Playing Cards, and Day Cards.

Eight **CHARACTER CARDS** can be made out of 4 × 6" plain index cards **cut in half cross-wise**. Type up the character information below and print out on printer labels or regular paper to cut and tape onto the cards:

Human	*Pod Person*
You can **erase** all hand-written cards.	You create the following cards:
What turns you into a Pod Person:	Pod cards Sleep cards
2 Pod cards 2 Sleep cards 1 Pod and 1 Sleep card	What **kills** you:
What **kills** you:	2 Flame Thrower cards
1 Suicide card	
(3 cards)	*(3 cards)*

<table>
<tr><td>

Doctor

You create the following cards:

Warning cards
(Ex: Jim is a Pod Person!)

What turns you into a Pod Person:

2 Pod cards

Sleep cards have no effect on you.

</td><td>

Pod Hunter

You create the following cards:

Flame Thrower cards

What turns you into a Pod Person:

2 Sleep cards

Pod cards have no effect on you.

</td></tr>
</table>

(1 card) *(1 card)*

To make 28 **PLAYING CARDS**, you'll also use 4 × 6" plain index cards **cut in half cross-wise**. Use printer labels or regular paper to cut and tape so that the cards state the following, leaving 17 of the cards **blank**:
- *Pod:* Used to turn Humans & the Doctor into Pod People. *(4 cards)*
- *Flame Thrower:* Used to kill Pod People. *(3 cards)*
- *Sleep:* Used to turn Humans & the Pod Hunter into Pod People. *(2 cards)*
- *Suicide:* Kills a Human. *(2 cards)*
- *(17 Blank cards)*

DAY CARDS will cause specific events to happen throughout the game. To make these cards, use 20 4 × 6" plain index cards that are **not** cut in half. Unless stated otherwise, make 1 of each Day card:
- One Day Passes *(10 cards)*
- *Double Up:* Each player passes 2 cards to another player instead of 1. *(2 cards)*
- *Get Rid of It:* Each player discards 1 card to the discard pile and gets a new playing card. *(2 cards)*
- *Rainy Day:* Any Human with 1 Sleep card in their hand becomes a Pod Person (except the Doctor).
- *Pod Bombs:* 1 Pod card in each player's hand has been bombed. Any passed pods do nothing this turn, and players suffer no effects as long as they get rid of them next turn.
- *Explosives:* Any Pod Person with **1** Flame Thrower in their hand is killed by its explosion.

- *Surrounded:* No warnings can be passed this turn. If a character has 2 warnings in their hand, 1 is erased and passed as blank.
- *Help When You Need It:* Each player can erase and write *any* type of card for this turn only. (Printed cards cannot be altered.)
- *You Gave Yourself Away:* Each player rolls the die. Whoever rolls the lowest number reveals their Character card (and admits if they have been changed).

PLAYING THE GAME

Place the Character cards, Playing cards and Day cards into separate piles. Day cards are shuffled and put **face down** in the center of the table with the die. The number of players determines the number of Character cards used:
- *5 players:* 1 Human, 1 Doctor, 1 Pod Hunter, 2 Pod People
- *6 players:* Add 1 Pod Person
- *7 players:* Add 1 Pod Person & 1 Human
- *8 players:* Add 1 Pod Person & 2 Humans

ROLES OF THE PLAYERS. Each player is given a Character card, 2 Playing cards and a pencil. Remaining Playing cards are kept face down in a pile. After looking at their Character cards, players keep them face down in front of them throughout the game (but may refer to them whenever they wish).

Each character in the game has a different role. Pod People will try to turn the Humans (including the Doctor and Pod Hunter) into other Pod People, and Humans will try to kill the Pod People. Each character is also affected differently by Playing cards, which is stated on their Character card:
- *2 Pod cards:* Turns a Human or the Doctor into a Pod Person.
- *2 Sleep cards:* Turns a Human or the Pod Hunter into a Pod Person.
- *1 Pod card + 1 Sleep card:* Turns a Human into a Pod Person.
- *2 Flame Thrower cards:* Kills a Pod Person.
- *Suicide card:* Kills a Human, but **not** the Doctor or the Pod Hunter.

BLANK CARDS are for players to write their *own* cards. (Printed Playing cards cannot be changed.) However, characters can only write specific cards, which are also listed on their Character cards:
- *Pod People:* Create Pod cards **and** Sleep cards.
- *Doctor:* Creates Warning cards (example: Jim is a Pod Person!).
- *Pod Hunter:* Creates Flame Thrower cards.
- *Humans:* Humans can only erase cards by drawing a line through what was previously written, passing it on to another player who they can only hope is a Human/Doctor/ Hunter. Humans **cannot** write new cards.

Players can **only** write new cards with blank cards that have not been written on before or have been erased by a Human.

SURVIVING THE GAME. At the beginning of each turn, a Day card is turned face up and the die is rolled. Unless the Day card states otherwise, players each give one card to another player, passing **clockwise** to player who sits the number of seats away as the number on the die. *(For example: rolling a 3 means players pass to the third person in the clockwise direction.)* Players do not pick up a new card from the main deck unless it is stated on the Day card to do so.

Although each player knows their own character, it remains a mystery who or what the other players are. Players pass cards while only *guessing* who is Human and who is a Pod Person. *In the first round of play, any dealt cards that would either kill or change a character have no effect.*

BECOMING A POD. Humans (including the Doctor and Pod Hunter) get turned into a Pod Person if **at any time** they hold cards in their hand that turn them into a Pod Person, which is listed on their Character card. When this happens, they must remember they are now a Pod Person, even though they have a different Character card. From the moment a Human/Pod Hunter/Doctor becomes a Pod Person, they can **only** write Pod and Sleep cards and can no longer perform actions of their previous character.

GETTING KILLED. Players may also die out of the game. This happens when a Human gets the Suicide card or when a Pod Person is killed by Flame Throwers. When a player is killed, they put their cards into a face down discard pile. They should not say what kind of character they were.

AFTER THE 20TH DAY. After Day 20, most of the players will be dead. Those still alive then turn their Character card **face up**, but keep their Playing cards hidden. If any have been changed into Pod People, they must admit it. Rather than rolling the die to see how cards are passed, remaining players choose who they pass cards to. This is done by rolling the die and the one who gets the highest number chooses first, and so on. Players only do this once and keep by the assigned order.

In addition, players each begin their turn by discarding a card and picking a new card from the remaining Playing cards. If players pick up a card that can either turn them into a Pod Person or kill them, it takes effect **immediately**. Once the deck of playing cards is gone through, the discard pile is shuffled and reused.

WINNING THE GAME. The game continues until all Humans are changed into Pod People or all the Pod People are dead. It may turn out that before Day 20, remaining players know that the others are the same type of character that they are — either Human or Pod People. If a player believes this is the case, he or she may turn their Character card over. The game is over if everyone is either one race or the other, or they continue to play until this is the case.

Tips

- Players should remember that just because they receive a particular card from a player, it doesn't necessarily mean that whoever gave it to them is a Pod Person or Human. They may just want to get that card out of their hand.

- Players can also "fake" being a particular character by pretending to erase a card or pretending to write something on a blank card.
- The Doctor should only write warnings about Pod People, not who is a Human. Remember that these cards may fall into the hands of Pod People.

MAKE THIS GAME YOUR OWN!

Make your version of You're Next! *original by drawing pictures on the Character cards and using fun fonts for the Day cards and Playing cards.*

LIKE THIS GAME?

Check out Surrounded *in Chapter 15 for another card game of man versus monster!*

You're Next!

Objects of the Game

Humans: Kill all the Pod People.
Pod People: Convert all the Humans into Pod People.

Players are each dealt a Character card and 2 Playing cards. Players look at their Character card and then keep it face down in front of them for the remainder of the game (but may refer to it whenever they wish). Remaining Playing cards are kept in a pile. Day cards are put face down in the center of the table with the die.

At the start of each turn, a Day card is turned over and the die is rolled. Unless stated otherwise on the card, players each pass 1 card clockwise to the number rolled on the die.

Players may create the following out of blank cards each turn:

Pod People: Pod Hunter:
Pod cards **and** Sleep cards   Flame Thrower cards

Doctor: Humans:
Warning cards   Draw a line through previously
                                                      written cards
                                        (Cannot write *new* cards)

Printed Playing cards cannot be changed.

Cards have the following effects on characters:
- *2 Pod cards:* Turns a Human or the Doctor into a Pod Person.
- *2 Sleep cards:* Turns a Human or the Pod Hunter into a Pod Person.
- *1 Pod card + 1 Sleep card:* Turns a Human into a Pod Person.
- *2 Flame Thrower cards:* Kills a Pod Person.
- *Suicide card:* Kills a Human, but **not** the Doctor or the Pod Hunter.
- *Warning card:* Warns Humans who specific Pod People are or might be.

If a Human is changed into a Pod Person, they must immediately follow all the rules of Pod People. *In the first round of play, any dealt cards that would either kill or change a character have no effect.*

GETTING KILLED. When a player dies out of the game, they put their cards in a face down discard pile, but do not reveal what type of character they were.

AFTER DAY 20, all Character cards are turned face up. If a player has been changed into a Pod Person, they must admit it. Each turn, players discard a card and pick a new playing card. They then **choose** who they distribute cards to, rolling the die and the highest number passing first. This is done once and players keep by the order.

WINNING THE GAME. The game ends when either all the Humans are changed into Pod People or all the Pod People are dead. If players believe that only their own characters are left in the game before Day 20, they may turn their Character card face up to see.

3
ORDER OF THE TRUE BELIEVER

Rune-Casting Journal Game
based on *Night of the Demon (1957)*,
3–8 players

Is the world of the supernatural a reality, or is it only in our minds? When surrounded by superstition and demonic beliefs, how long could you go before starting to see things that defy explanation, until doubting your own conviction of what is real?

Night of the Demon is a classic thriller that puts belief in the occult to the ultimate test with ancient runes, parapsychology, satanic cults and monstrous myths. This race against the fates turns deadly when black and white magic come together and even the skeptics can't leave any room for chance.

THE GAME

In this rune-casting journal game, players assume the roles of cult members of The Order of the True Believer, engaging in a little game that could mean their lives. Each uses a journal of occult studies to read a true message of the runes, escape an ancient demon and hope to outlive fellow cult members with each cast. You will need:

- 24 Elder Futhark runes with Casting Bag   • Small Blank Journal **for each Player**
- Pen **for each Player**   • Sheet of Tan or Brown Paper   • Small Bowl
- Scissors   • Double-Sided Tape   • Highlighter

PREPARING THE GAME

To make Order of the True Believer, you'll need to prepare the following: Occult Journal **for each Player**, Strip of Parchment **for each Journal**, Rune Symbolism Sheet **for each Player**

The **OCCULT JOURNALS** are filled with subjects that members of the Order of the True Believer both believe and study. Photocopy the journal pages below so you have one complete set for each player, then cut and tape them into small journals or sketch books, keeping the pages in the same order in each journal.

Strips of **PARCHMENT** will be used to determine which player could be the next one killed by the demon conjured during the game. Cut a piece of tan or brown paper into 2 × 6" strips, then draw the rune symbols shown below on **one** of the strips and leave the rest blank. Fold each parchment strip in half and place one inside each journal.

SYMBOLISM SHEETS. Photocopy the Rune Symbolism sheet so there is one for each player. (The first page will be a half-page.) These sheets will help players interpret their rune casts each turn. Use a highlighter to highlight the Perthro symbol on each sheet.

PLAYING THE GAME

Each player begins the game with a journal, pen and Rune Symbolism sheet. Place the small bowl and bag of runes in the middle of the table. Throughout the game, players will cast runes to foresee their true futures. Points can be gained or lost each turn depending on which runes are cast. However, players also risk their lives in playing, as an ancient demon from the underworld is conjured when a certain rune is cast. Whichever player holds the parchment of runes is doomed to be the next victim of the demon — unless they can get rid of the paper before it appears.

THE DIVINE CAST. The game begins by each player taking 3 runes from the rune bag and laying them out from left to right. Players should **take turns** doing this, so that they choose from all 24 runes. This first cast represents the player's Divine Cast, which will give them 5 points if they should ever cast it again throughout the game, and can even bring them back from the dead if they die out of the game. The divine cast is sketched on the second page of each player's journal, beneath the Divine Cast heading.

The runes are then put back into the bag. Remaining turns consist of turning to a journal page (starting with the Pentagram page), reading the topic aloud and each player taking three runes **at once**.

CASTING THE RUNES. The cast runes are once again laid out from left to right. The left rune represents something from the player's **past**. The middle rune represents a **current situation**. The right rune represents the **future** of this situation if their current path continues. At the bottom of their journal page, players draw the symbol of their runes and briefly describe their meanings in a few words, which should be taken from their Symbolism sheet. Players may alter the wording for the same rune cast more than once.

Example journal entry:

Inspiration
Reward, happiness
Positive changes

Once everyone has finished their journal entries, players announce their casts to the group. Depending on their runes, players may gain or lose points, as described below.

POINTS. Players gain or lose points depending on their casts and the current journal page. Some journal pages are safe and can give points while others are dangerous and can make players lose points. If a player casts a rune listed on the bottom left-hand corner of a **positive** journal page (with a talisman), they get 2 points for each listed rune. If they cast **no** runes listed on a positive journal page, they get no points. If they cast a rune listed on a **negative** journal page (with a skeleton), they get 1 point for each listed rune. If they cast **no** runes listed on a negative journal page, they **lose** 1 point. If at any time a player casts *the same rune in the same order* more than once, they get a point. For example, if they cast Isa for their future (third) on the first page and then Isa again for their future on the fifth page, they get a point on the fifth page for casting Isa twice in the same order.

Accumulated points will help players win the game, but can also help them stay alive. Each time a player gets **2 or more** points on any turn, they have the option to get rid of their parchment strip. This is done by each player putting their parchment into the bowl, shuffling them around and choosing a new one.

PERTHRO RUNE. Each time Perthro is cast, players mark the top of their Symbolism sheet. The **third** time Perthro is cast **since the last parchment swap**, the demon has been summoned and kills whoever is holding the parchment of symbols. If the player with the symbols gains 2 points when the third Perthro comes up, it is too late: the demon has already struck.

DEAD PLAYERS. After a player is killed, one of the blank parchment strips is removed from the game and the rest are put in the bowl for the surviving players to choose from. Dead players can still take part in the game, but they neither accumulate nor lose any points and any Perthro runes they cast have no effect. Players can only come back to life if they cast their Divine cast *after* they have been killed.

CASTING THE DIVINE CAST. If a player casts their Divine Cast while alive, they receive 5 points and have the option for the rune papers to be swapped. If they cast their Divine Cast while dead, they receive no points from it but are back in the game and can once again accumulate and lose points.

WINNING THE GAME. The game continues with players casting runes each turn and using their journal pages in the same order. The game ends when **half** of the players are dead *or* all the pages have been gone through and surviving player with the most points wins. (When playing with an odd number of players, the amount of players to die is rounded up.)

READING THE TRUE MESSAGE. Once the game is over, players should look through their journals to see which runes were cast the most often *in each order*: past, present and future. This will be their overall message of the runes.

Tips

- Elder Futhark runes can be found at just about any New Age shop or website for an average cost of $20. In addition to the original 24 runes, many sets also include a blank rune, which is not needed for this game.

LIKE THIS GAME?

Check out Hell and Damnation *in Chapter 14 for another journal game of life and death!*

Order of the True Believer
Object of the Game

Cast the runes to see your past, present and future —
and outlive your fellow cult members!

Each player is given a journal of cult studies, Rune Symbolism sheet and pen. Journals contain a strip of parchment: one containing a series of runes, the rest blank. A small bowl and bag of runes are put in the center of the table.

DIVINE CAST. Each player chooses 3 of all 24 runes for their Divine Cast. The symbols are drawn on the second page of the journals under Divine Cast.

REMAINING CASTS. Players turn to the next page of their journal and read the information aloud. Each turn, **all players** take 3 runes from the bag and lay them out from left to right, writing the symbols and basic meanings of their cast at the bottom of their journal page. *Example: Inspiration; Reward, happiness; Positive changes.* Pages are played in order.

POINTS. Players may gain or lose points depending on their cast and current journal page:

- **Positive** Pages: (talisman)
  - Each listed rune cast: Gain 2 pts.
  - No listed runes cast: 0 pts.
- **Negative** Pages: (skeleton)
  - Each listed rune cast: Gain 1 pt.
  - No listed runes cast: Lose 1 pt.
- 2+ Points on a Turn: Player has the option to get rid of their parchment. Papers are put in the bowl, shuffled, and each player picks one.
- Repeated Cast: If at any time a player casts *the same rune in the same order* more than once in the game, they get a point.
- Divine Cast: Gives 5 points. If the player has died out of the game, the Divine Cast brings them back to life (but does not give them 5 points).

PERTHRO. Each time Perthro is cast, players mark the top of their Symbolism sheet. The third time Perthro is cast **since the last parchment swap**, the demon is summoned and kills whomever holds the parchment of symbols. If the player with the symbols gains 2 points when the third Perthro comes up, it is too late: the demon has already struck.

DEAD PLAYERS. When a player is killed, one of the blank parchments is removed and the rest are put into the bowl for surviving players to choose from. Dead players can still take part in the game, but can neither accumulate nor lose points and any Perthro runes they cast have no effect. Players can only come back to life if they cast their Divine cast *after* they have been killed, and may continue to gain or lose points on their next turn.

WINNING THE GAME. The game ends when **half** of the players are dead *or* all the pages have been gone through and the surviving player with the most points wins. *(When playing with an odd number of players, the amount of players to die is rounded up.)*

READING YOUR TRUE RUNES. After the game, players should look through their journals for which runes were cast the most often in each order: past, present and future. This will be their overall message of the runes.

COPY @ 120%

ORDER OF THE TRUE BELIEVER

"Evil is good, and good, evil.
In the joy of sin will mankind, that is lost,
find itself again."

Casting the Runes

Draw 3 runes and lay them
out from left to right.

Left: Past
Center: Situation you currently face
Right: Future outcome of current situation

DIVINE CAST:
Gives 5 points if cast while alive.
Also brings player back from the dead.

Past * Present Situation * Future

Pentagram

A five-pointed star drawn within a circle.

Each of the 5 points of the pentagram represents the 5 elements:
Air, Water, Earth, Fire, Spirit.

When the pentagram is drawn with 1 point down, it is used to call forth the powers of evil. Drawn with 2 points down, it is used as a power to banish evil and bring good luck.

Runes: *Reading:*   *Points:*

Demons

Malevolent spirits that may be conjured and insecurely controlled. They are jealous of humans for being favored by God.

Demons offer gifts and pleasures to humans with the final intention of destroying their souls, and may even take over their bodies and kill them.

Runes: *Reading:*   *Points:*

COPY @ 120%

The Evil Eye

A look of envy from someone with the Evil Eye can bring harm to people, livestock or a possession.

Some believe the power of the Evil Eye is deliberate, while others hold that it is inborn, unconscious and automatic.

Talismans are often used to ward off its effects.

Runes: *Reading:*   *Points:*

The Magic Circle

A barrier of magically effective words and symbols drawn on the floor to surround a magician during rituals and provide protection against hostile spirits and forces.

When a magician summons a demon, he is safe as long as he stays inside the circle. If he breaks the circle, the demon can kill him.

Runes: *Reading:*   *Points:*

Necromancy

The art of conjuring the souls of the dead to use
for spiritual protection or personal gain.

Medieval necromancy involved magic circles, conjurations
and sacrifices as payment for summoning.

Runes: *Reading:*   *Points:*

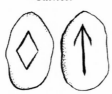

Lucifer

The chief of angels who rebelled against God, mistakenly
applied to the Christian Devil.

Lucifer (Latin for "light bearer") represents the temptation
of intellectual arrogance with its tendency to retreat from
material existence into a purely mental life.

Runes: *Reading:*   *Points:*

COPY @ 120%

The Incubus & The Succubus

Incubus: A male demon that visits women to have sex
with them in their sleep.
Succubus: A female demon that visits men.

Both demons gravitate towards those who have vowed
a celibate life.

Runes:　　　　*Reading:*　　　　*Points:*

The Witching Hour

Midnight: The time when witches, demons
and ghosts are most powerful and black
magic is most effective.

The Witching Hour can also be referred to
midnight during a full moon.

Runes:

Reading:　　　　*Points:*

Elemental Spirits

Spirits inhabiting one of four magical elements. They have limited intelligence but extensive powers over the element they indwell. Their powers are at the disposal of their conjurer.

Runes: *Reading:*   *Points:*

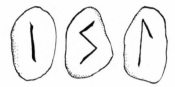

The Seven Deadly Sins

Sins which threaten eternal damnation when committed. Each is believed to be tempted by a specific demon:

Lust: Asmodeus   *Pride:* Lucifer
Greed: Mammon   *Envy:* Leviathan
Gluttony: Beelzebub   *Sloth:* Belphegor
Wrath: Satan

Runes: *Reading:*   *Points:*

The Seven Hells

In Cabalistic lore, seven Hells are located in the sixth of the seven Earths.
The first Hell is closest to the surface of the earth,
and the seventh is the farthest down.

1. Gehenna
2. Tzelmoth
3. Shaare Moth
4. Tit ha-Yon

5. Bar Shachath
6. Abbadon
7. Sheol

Runes: *Reading:*   *Points:*

The Black Candle

The use of candles in magic involves colored symbolism:
black for cursing and banishing, red for sexual desire, green for money,
and white for spirituality and healing.

Ceremonial candles are anointed with oils, and sometimes rearranged on an
alter to represent an intended rearrangement in the world.

Runes: *Reading:*   *Points:*

Sacrifice

An exchange of gifts between the gods and
humanity to ensure fertile crops and livestock.

Offerings usually consist of valuables, livestock or — in some
cases — humans, made at the alter of one or more gods.

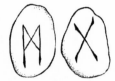

Runes: *Reading:*   *Points:*

Talisman

A small amulet or other object, often bearing
magical symbols, worn around the neck
for protection against evil spirits.

The material basis of the talisman forms a
body for energies placed within it at the time
of consecration. After used in ceremony,
they must be deconsecrated and destroyed.

Runes: *Reading:*   *Points:*

Pact with the Devil

An oral contract or one written in blood in which the devil gives youth, money or power in exchange for a person's soul. Such pacts can be made with demons as well as devils, both of which are summoned by one in desperate need.

A mark is usually inflicted on the person to be used as proof the deal was made.

Runes: *Reading:*   *Points:*

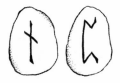

Rune Symbolism Sheet

 Fehu   Prosperity, luck. Earned income, possessions won or earned.

 Uruz   Untamed potential. Freedom, energy, action, courage, strength.

 Thurisaz   A tendency toward change. A reactive or directed force of defense or conflict.

 Ansuz   Communication, inspiration or enthusiasm. A revealing message of wisdom.

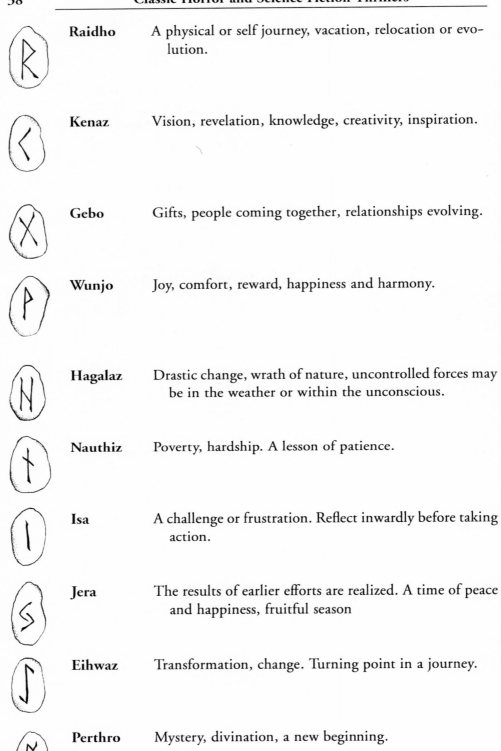

	Raidho	A physical or self journey, vacation, relocation or evolution.
	Kenaz	Vision, revelation, knowledge, creativity, inspiration.
	Gebo	Gifts, people coming together, relationships evolving.
	Wunjo	Joy, comfort, reward, happiness and harmony.
	Hagalaz	Drastic change, wrath of nature, uncontrolled forces may be in the weather or within the unconscious.
	Nauthiz	Poverty, hardship. A lesson of patience.
	Isa	A challenge or frustration. Reflect inwardly before taking action.
	Jera	The results of earlier efforts are realized. A time of peace and happiness, fruitful season
	Eihwaz	Transformation, change. Turning point in a journey.
	Perthro	Mystery, divination, a new beginning.

COPY @ 120%

	Algiz	Resist temptation. Defense or guard for warding off evil.
	Sowilo	Positive energy and changes. The life-force, health.
	Tiwaz	Duty, discipline, leadership. Analysis and rationality.
	Berkano	New beginnings, both mental and physical growth. Abundance.
	Ehwaz	Transportation and communication. Movement and change for the better.
	Mannaz	The Self; family, community and relationships. Your attitude toward others and their attitudes towards you.
	Laguz	Intuition and mystery, imagination and psychic matters. Hidden sources of creativity.
	Ingwaz	Completion of ideas or projects. Rest stage, a time of relief and no anxiety.
	Dagaz	Balance and connection. Awakening and clarity.
	Othala	Spiritual wealth. Inherited property or possessions, a house, a home.

COPY @ 120%

4

THE WRONG EXPERIMENT

Experiment Decoding Game
based on *The Fly (1958)*,
3–8 players

The Fly is a science fiction thriller that just may haunt your dreams forever. Research scientist Dr. Andre Delmbre may have good intentions with his experiments to benefit the world, but he soon discovers the dire consequences of tampering with the laws of nature.

A film as heart-wrenching as it is horrific, we find ourselves pitying the Fly as much as we fear him, remaining on the edge of our seats while a distraught family does all they can to reverse an experiment gone horribly wrong.

THE GAME

In this game of scientific formulas and self-mutilation, players find themselves horribly mutated after a terrible experiment, their lives now in the hands of their teammates to reverse the process. Experiments will vary with each player, as will the results as each failed attempt to save them leads to lab destructions, mental trauma and death. You will need:

- 15 3 × 5" Plain Index Cards • 7 Plastic Flies or Other Insects
- Scrap Paper **for each Player** • Pen **for each Player** • Egg Timer • Stapler

PREPARING THE GAME

To make *The Wrong Experiment*, you'll need to put together the following: Lab Books and Experiment Cards

LAB BOOKS. Photocopy the Lab Book below so that there is one book for each player. A sample Lab Book is also provided to show how the books are used in the game.

EXPERIMENT CARDS. Next, make 15 Experiment cards out of 3 × 5" plain index cards. Write one formula, machine or source of energy from the Lab Books on each card so that they resemble the following:

The Speed of Light $(3 \times 10^8$ m/s$)$	**Nuclear Reactor**	**Lead Acid Battery**

PLAYING THE GAME

Each player begins the game with a Lab Book, piece of scrap paper and pen. Place the Experiment cards face up in the center of the table along with the timer and plastic flies.

PERFORMING THE EXPERIMENT. Players assume the roles of scientists who have been conducting secret experiments on themselves. To begin, each fills out the Lab Experiment Sheet of their Lab Book to describe the experiment they have performed as well as its results: both good and bad. Experiments can be one of any nature, and sample experiments are listed.

Next, players turn to the Results Sheet of their Lab Book and check off 6 items they used in the experiment. Each item contains specific results from past experiments and has a blank line underneath it. Players should choose their 6 items based on the purpose of their experiment and on the blank lines write **3 new** results that occurred: 2 results that went wrong and 1 result that went right. In addition, players should write "Death" on 3 items they did **not** use in their experiment. These items may kill the player when used incorrectly. Finally, players should write "Bang!" on 1 item they did **not** use in their experiment. This item will result in a lab explosion when used incorrectly.

BECOMING THE FLY. After everyone has filled out their Lab Book, one player volunteers to be the first who suffered a mutation during their experiment and became a human fly. The player begins by taking the seven plastic flies and scattering them around the room while the others keep their eyes closed. The flies should be put in areas so they are visible, but a good distance apart. The player — who is now the Fly — returns to the table and writes one **key word** from the purpose of their experiment on their scrap paper. *(For example, if they performed an experiment to make themselves psychic, the key word could be "psychic.")*

REVERSING THE EXPERIMENT. It is now up to the other players to try and **reverse** the experiment that transformed the player into a fly. To do this, they must acquire a fly and figure out the exact formula the player used in their original experiment. To do this, the Fly (player) writes Day 1 on their scrap paper and sets the timer for 2 minutes. One other player must then search the room for one of the flies. If they don't find a fly in that time, the experiment has failed because the fly got away.

When they do find a fly, the player then chooses 6 different items from their Lab Book that they think the Fly may have used in their experiment. Their choices should be based on the key word the Fly wrote and the information about each item on the Results Sheet. The player then takes the 6 Experiment cards of the chosen items and puts them in the center of the table. The Fly consults his or her Lab Book to see if it the experiment is successful.

FAILED EXPERIMENTS. If the 6 cards are **not** the exact items the Fly used, the experiment fails and the Fly does the following:
- *New Results:* If any of the 3 new results were chosen, the Fly puts **one** of the new results cards face up in front of them, where it is kept for the remainder of the game. They also write the new result from their sheet on their scrap paper for further clues of the experiment. Players now only need to choose the remaining 5 items to reverse the experiment. (The Fly only admits 1 new result each turn, even if more than 1 were played.) Once all 3 of the new results have been chosen, the Fly reads their Lab Experiment Sheet aloud.
- *Death Items:* If **2 or more** of the death items were chosen, the Fly takes **1** and puts it **face down** in front of them for the remainder of the game. If the 2 remaining death items are chosen on a single turn, the Fly dies. *The Fly does this in addition to writing any new results.*
- *Lab Explosion:* If the item that causes a lab explosion has been chosen, the lab explodes and the flies scatter. Remaining players have only 1 minute to find a fly at the start of their turn. The Fly does not admit which item caused this, and any future uses of the item result in losing an additional 10 seconds for finding a fly. *This is done in addition to writing any new results and removing a death card.*

If neither new results, death items nor a lab explosion has been chosen, the Fly removes one of the incorrect cards used.

Players can work together, but only one player should make the ultimate decision for the items in the experiment each turn. Players have a total of **7 tries** at locating flies and performing experiments before it is too late for the Fly to return to normal again, and he or she loses their mind for good.

EXPERIMENT REVERSAL OR DEATH. The game continues with each player taking on the role as the new Fly, hiding the plastic flies around the room and hoping to be once again returned to human form.

Tips

- If you can't locate a bag of flies at your local party supply store, you can also use other forms of insects in the game, such as plastic spiders or other bugs.

MAKE THIS GAME YOUR OWN!

Make your version of The Wrong Experiment *unique by tearing up the edges of the Lab Notebooks and scratching up the covers as if they had fallen into the hands of the Fly. You can also draw images on the cover sheets and Experiment cards, such as flies, beakers and test tubes.*

The Wrong Experiment

Object of the Game

Reverse the experiment that caused your fellow scientist to turn into a fly.

PERFORMING EXPERIMENTS. Players fill out their Lab Experiment Sheets to explain an experiment they performed on themselves. On the Results Sheet 6 items are checked off that were used in the experiment and reflect its purpose and results. Of the 6 items used, 3 **new** results are written on the blank lines underneath: 2 results that went wrong and 1 result that went right. "Death" is written underneath 3 items that were **not** used in the experiment, and "Bang!" is written for another unused item.

THE FLY. One player volunteers to be the first Fly. They hide 7 plastic flies throughout the room while the others keep their eyes closed. They scribble on the scrap paper **1 key word** to describe their experiment.

EACH TURN. The Fly writes Day 1, 2, etc. on their paper. A timer is set for 2 minutes, and 1 player searches the room for a fly. Failure to find a fly results in a **failed** experiment. If a fly is found, the player chooses 6 items from the Lab Book that may match those originally used in the experiment, hoping to reverse the process and make the Fly human again. Players base their guesses on the key word from the Fly's scrap paper and the information about items on the Results Sheet. They put the Experiment cards of the chosen items in the middle of the table. The Fly looks at the Results Sheet to see if the experiment is successful.

EXPERIMENT RESULTS. If the 6 cards are not the exact items the Fly used, the experiment fails and The Fly does the following:

- *New Results:* If any of the new results were chosen, the Fly puts **1** new result card face up in front of them, where it stays for the remainder of the game. They write the new result from their sheet on their scrap paper. (Players now only need 5 items to reverse the experiment.) Only 1 new result can be admitted each turn. Once all 3 of the new results have been chosen, the Fly reads their Lab Experiment Sheet aloud.
- *Death Items:* If **2 or more** of the death items were chosen, the Fly takes 1 and puts it **face down** for the remainder of the game. If the 2 remaining death items are chosen on a single turn, the Fly dies. *The Fly does this in addition to writing any new results.*
- *Lab Explosion:* If the item that causes a lab explosion is chosen, the lab explodes and the flies scatter. Remaining players have **1 minute** to find a fly as they begin their turn. The Fly does not admit which item caused this; future uses of the item result in losing an additional 10 seconds for finding a fly. *This is done in addition to writing any new results and removing a death card.*

If nothing new results, death items nor a lab explosion has been chosen, the Fly removes one of the incorrect cards used.

EXPERIMENT REVERSAL OR DEATH. The game continues until The Fly is changed back to normal with the correct 6 items chosen or 7 days (turns) go by without a successful experiment, in which time the Fly loses its mind for good and dies.

The Wrong Experiment

Lab Book

LAB EXPERIMENT SHEET

Provide the details of your most recent experiment in which you
used yourself as a guinea pig.

Name: _____

Date of Experiment: _____

Purpose of Experiment: _____

_____

_____

Results: _____

_____

_____

*Sample Experiments Performed
by Fellow Mad Scientists*

The Power of Invisibility

The Power to Change One's Appearance

The Power to Heal Oneself

The Power to See in the Dark

The Power to Make Bones as Strong as Steel

The Power to be Lightweight and Fly

The Power to Walk through Walls

The Power to Run with Incredible Speed

COPY @ 120%

SAMPLE LAB EXPERIMENT SHEET

Provide the details of your most recent experiment in which you used yourself as a guinea pig.

Name: _____Chris_____

Date of Experiment: _July 16_____

Purpose of Experiment: _To unlock areas of the brain that cause psychic abilities_

_____

_____

Results: _Uncontrollable perception of others' thoughts, vivid memory_

_flashbacks, headaches, nosebleeds_____

_____

Sample Experiments Performed by Fellow Mad Scientists

The Power of Invisibility

The Power to Change One's Appearance

The Power to Heal Oneself

The Power to See in the Dark

The Power to Make Bones as Strong as Steel

The Power to be Lightweight and Fly

The Power to Walk through Walls

The Power to Run with Incredible Speed

RESULTS SHEET

Mark 6 items you used in your experiment.
Write 3 new results among them:
2 results that went *wrong*, and 1 that went *right*.
Write "Death" on 3 items not used in the experiment.
Write "Bang!" on 1 item not used in the experiment.

Mathematical Formulas

The Speed of Light
$(3 \times 10^8$ m/s)

Makes objects appear lighter in color; enhances strength of the pupils

---

Ohm's Law
$(J = \sigma E)$

Advances regeneration capabilities; reduced resistance to gravity

---

Theory of Relativity
$(E = mc^2)$

Rearrangement of bodily atoms; enhanced energy output

Area of a Circle
(πr^2)

Enhances strength in the eyes; increases bodily strength

Avogadro's Number
(6.022×10^{23})

Strengthened sense of hearing; increase in brain activity

Machines

Nuclear Reactor

Alters reflection of light from the eyes; ability to alter surrounding matter

---

Mass Spectrometer

Produces pigment alteration; increase in bone and joint growth

---

Nuclear Magnetic Resource Imager

Alters shape of the eyeball; alters body mass distribution

Computer Tomography Scanner

Strengthens white blood cells; enhances blood flow

Polymerase Chain Reaction Machine

Enhances bodily flexibility; quickens the body's metabolism

Sources of Energy

Lead Acid Battery

Increase in protein levels; unstable mental processes

Fossil Fuel

Heightened sensitivity to surroundings; increased buoyancy

Wind Mill Generator

Produces skin tissue alteration; increase in red blood cells

Lightning Rod

Severe aggression; alters the pigment of the eyes

Thermal Energy

Tolerance to extreme temperatures; alters the body's reflection of light

SAMPLE RESULTS SHEET

Mark 6 items you used in your experiment.
Write 3 new results among them:
2 results that went *wrong*, and 1 that went *right*.
Write "Death" on 3 items not used in the experiment.
Write "Bang!" on 1 item not used in the experiment.

Mathematical Formulas	*Machines*	*Sources of Energy*
The Speed of Light $(3 \times 10^8 \text{ m/s})$ Makes objects appear lighter in color; enhances strength of the pupils *Death*	**Nuclear Reactor** Alters reflection of light from the eyes; ability to alter surrounding matter *Death*	**Lead Acid Battery** Increase in protein levels; unstable mental processes
Ohm's Law $(J = \sigma E)$ Advances regeneration capabilities; reduced resistance to gravity *Memory Flashbacks*	**Mass Spectrometer** Produces pigment alteration; increase in bone and joint growth	**Fossil Fuel** Heightened sensitivity to surroundings; increased buoyancy
Theory of Relativity $(E = mc^2)$ Rearrangement of bodily atoms; enhanced energy output	**Nuclear Magnetic Resource Imager** Alters shape of the eyeball; alters body mass distribution *Headaches*	**Wind Mill Generator** Produces skin tissue alteration; increase in red blood cells *Bang!*
Area of a Circle (πr^2) Enhances strength in the eyes; increases bodily strength *Death*	**Computer Tomography Scanner** Strengthens white blood cells; enhances blood flow	**Lightning Rod** Severe aggression; alters the pigment of the eyes
Avogadro's Number (6.022×10^{23}) Strengthened sense of hearing; increase in brain activity	**Polymerase Chain Reaction Machine** Enhances bodily flexibility; quickens the body's metabolism	**Thermal Energy** Tolerance to extreme temperatures; alters the body's reflection of light *Psychic Abilities*

5
THE NIGHTLY HAUNT

Murder Mystery Game
based on *House on Haunted Hill (1959)*,
6–12 players

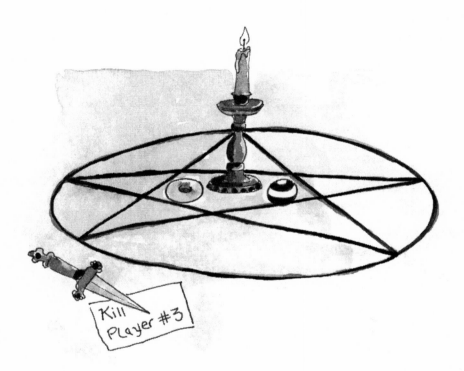

House on Haunted Hill is a classic ghost story and murder mystery all in one. A dry-humored millionaire — played by the one and only Vincent Price — has invited a few guests to spend the night in a rented mansion for a reward of $10,000. There is a rumor that the place is haunted — but then again, it may be all a hoax. Either way, once the visitors decide they are up for the challenge, there's no turning back, as everyone is locked in for the night, and each with a deadly weapon. The only way to survive until daybreak: watch out for ghosts, watch the clock, and watch your back.

THE GAME

In this murder mystery party, you follow in Frederick Loren's footsteps and invite people to spend the evening at a haunted house you have "rented" for the night. Anyone who survives until midnight receives $10,000 (a fake check which reads "*I survived the House on Haunted Hill!*"). But this is not just any house, it's reportedly haunted by its former residents, some of whom were nice, and some who were not.

Unlike other murder mystery games which involve players taking on specific character roles, both you and your guests attend the party just as you are, but soon find yourself involved in a series of deadly tasks. You will need:

- 3–4 Dark and Deadly Prizes • 2 Pieces of Black Cardstock
- Blank Name Tag **for each Player** • Small Notebook **for each Player**
- Noose with a Blank Index Card attached **for each Player** • Digital Camera
- Pen **for each Player** • Small Black Gift Bag • Small Purple Gift Bag
- Small Red Gift Bag

Weapons: • 2 Fake Hand Guns • 2 Vials of Poison (Water) • 2 Fake Knives
- 2 Index Cards reading "Chandelier Falls" • 2 Nooses

Décor & Clues: * • 2 Crucifixes • Fake Skull, Body Parts and Skeleton Bones
- Black Robe • Witch Mask • Gem Necklace • Spider Webs • Baby Toys
- Cheesecloth • Pictures/Statues of Demons and Devils • Book of Devil Worship
- Black Candle • White Candle • Black Stones • Pentagram • Chalk
- Records from the 1940s • Vial of Fake Blood • Carpet with Red Stain

PREPARING THE GAME

To set up your Nightly Haunt party, prepare the following: Photocopied Invites and Clues, Number Tags, Floor Cards, Decor.

PHOTOCOPIED INVITES AND CLUES. Photocopy each of the following invitations and clues, all of which can be found at the end of this chapter:

- *Invitations:* Mail one invitation to each guest, keeping one for yourself for the night of the party.
- *Notes:* Photocopy each set of Notes: *Murder Notes, Secrets, Dinner Notes* and *Further Intentions*. Cut the notes into individual strips and put them in the following bags:
  - *Secrets:* Small **black** bag
  - *Dinner Notes:* Small **purple** bag
  - *Further Intentions*: Small **red** bag
  - *Murder Notes:* Shuffle these notes and split them between the **red** and **black** bags
- *Isabelle's Secret Spell:* Photocopy or handwrite the secret spell on old fashioned paper

*Décor items will vary with background story.

and write "To Bring me Back" at the top with a red marker. Place the spell on the altar in the basement (discussed in the Décor section below).

- *Letter from the Antique Dealer:* Photocopy or handwrite the letter on off-white paper to place on a nightstand in the bedroom.
- *Checks:* Photocopy the fake checks so there is one for each player.
- *Host Sheets:* The Host Sheets contain everything you'll need to explain the game to the guests and keep it moving step by step. Keep your Host Sheets and invitation together.

NUMBER TAGS. Players may not be assuming character roles in the game, but they *will* need a way to identify each other to perform certain secret tasks. This is done by assigning players specific numbers. Write Player 1, Player 2, etc. on name tags so there is one numbered tag for each player.

FLOOR CARDS. At one point in the game, players will be assigned a specific floor of the house to search for clues. This will be done with Floor Cards. To make the Floor cards, photocopy the cards below and attach each to a 3 × 3.5" piece of black cardstock. You'll need one Floor card for each player.

DÉCOR. The décor for your haunted house and murder mystery will bring your background story to life, providing clues as to whether the house is really haunted or if it's just a hoax, as well as traces of the previous occupants. Use the following examples for setting up props and clues throughout any and all of the rooms in your house where guests will be free to roam. Shut the doors of any rooms that will not be used in the game.

Entranceway   • Spider webs stretched in ceiling corners
- A black robe hanging from a coat hook
- *Weapon: "Chandelier Falls" card*

Kitchen   • A severed head or skull in an open cabinet
- A large piece of cheesecloth over the table
- White candle and book of matches
- Small vials of blood on the counter
- *Weapon: Knife*

Living Room   • Torn cheesecloth over the curtains
- A book of devil worship and pentagram on the coffee table
- Lit candles on end tables
- A few records from the 1940s
- *Weapon: Noose*

Stairway   • A crucifix turned upside down on the wall
- Stretched spider webbing in between the railings
- A carpet at the bottom of the stairs with a large red stain
- *Weapon: Gun*

Hallway • A dozen bones lining the wall
- A noose with a blank index card attached for each player on the wall
- *Weapon: "Chandelier Falls" card*

Bedroom • A witch (stuffed dummy) sitting up in bed with a gem necklace around its neck
- Devil/Demon statues or pictures on a dresser
- Letter from the Antiques Dealer on the nightstand
- *Weapon: Noose*

Spare Room • Circle of baby toys on the floor
- "Joshua" written in chalk inside the toy circle
- Isabelle's Secret Spell
- A bible and crucifix on a small table
- *Weapon: Poison*

Bathroom • A hand in the sink
- A skull surrounded by tea-light candles on a shelf
- Picture of the Devil or demon on the wall
- *Weapon: Knife*

Basement • A small altar containing Isabelle's spell, black candles and black stones
- Scattered bones around the alter
- A pentagram drawn in chalk on the floor with a baby toy inside it
- *Weapon: Poison and Gun*

REAL OR HOAX?

If you want the haunting of your House on Haunted Hill to be true, set up the items as they are. If you want to create an atmosphere that suggests the haunting is a *hoax*, leave clues of fraudulence, as well. Put a bottle of food coloring near the stained carpet, a modern-day piece of jewelry in the pentagram in the basement and a "How to Haunt Your House" book sticking out from under a bed. These clues shouldn't be next to *each* piece of décor, but scattered about so that only some of the players will put the pieces together.

PLAYING THE GAME

Before the guests arrive, make sure all your clues and weapons are in their proper places, checking off the list in the Décor section as you go. In addition, lay out the notebooks, pens and digital camera in the living room for players to use if they wish. Keep the *Secrets* bag within reach, but hide the other two bags of secret notes.

Once everyone has arrived, read the Host Sheet which includes a letter written by you (the host) and explains the nature of the party. Everyone will soon find that even though they have been challenged to spend the night surviving a series of ghosts, there are many other factors that may prevent them from seeing the light of day again.

IDENTITIES AND MISSIONS. Once you've read the rules, shuffle and distribute a number tag to each player, assigning them as Player 1, 2, 3, etc. Players should wear their tags for the remainder of the game.

Each player then chooses one note from the *Secrets* bag. These notes will give specific instructions to carry out before the night is over. As host, you should also choose a number tag and note. *(If a player chooses a note that deals with their own character, they must choose again.)*

STAYING ALIVE. Throughout the evening, players must fulfill the tasks on their secret notes if they hope to win the game. Everyone is given time to explore the house before dinner for a variety of reasons, such as looking for evidence of ghosts, looking for evidence of the haunting being a hoax, trying to bring a witch back from the dead, or trying to kill each other. Encourage players to write down any clues they come across or suspicions they have of other players. While exploring the house, players will also come across deadly weapons they may use to kill other players.

THE KILL. With each player that gets killed off, the reward money goes **up**. Players kill one another by showing a weapon or weapon card to another player when they are alone together. Players may choose to either take a weapon they come across and hold onto it or use it on the spot and then leave it. Players may only take one weapon at a time and should not hide weapons throughout the house. Those being killed should not scream or make any noise to call attention to their killer, as the killer would most likely smother them or kill them too quickly for any struggle.

When a player is killed, they quietly put any weapons or other items from the game they were holding on the floor where they died. They then take a noose from the wall, write on the card how they were killed (hanged, shot, stabbed, poisoned or chandelier fall) and wear the noose for the remainder of the game. From this point on, the player should not speak about anything related to the game, including how they were killed. (The dead player can still talk throughout the evening, of course, but they cannot talk about anything happening in the game, such as revealing who killed them.)

One important rule is that players should not kill anyone unless their secret note tells them to do so *or* if they witness a player kill someone else, and therefore kill that player to keep themselves and the others safe. This is why it is so important that players **not get caught** killing someone. (However, players *are* allowed to accuse others of being a murderer to try to get other players to believe them.) Any players who kill someone for no reason are disqualified and receive no money or prizes at the end.

OTHER MOTIVES. Players may find their secret notes have nothing to do with killing another player, but rather instruct them to prove the existence of ghosts, debunk it, acquire money, or simply hide in the crowd. The wide variety of motives in the game is what will prevent anyone from knowing who to trust.

DINNER. After searching the house for clues, dinner is served. As everyone sits down, the bag of *Dinner Notes* is passed around and each player takes a note. These notes instruct them to either do or say something to the player (who is still alive) sitting next to them.

During dinner, players should also discuss their intentions of the evening: to prove or disprove the existence of ghosts or simply to get the money and run. Players always have the option to lie about their motives or be completely honest. However, players should not reveal their notes at any time. If anyone has been killed in the game so far, players should also discuss who the killer may be.

FURTHER INTENTIONS. After dinner, players will be asked if they have found any clues around the house that may be connected to its former occupants. If either the antique dealer's letter or the spell has been uncovered, the player will read it aloud, as others may wish to use it to their advantage.

Each player then chooses a final note from the red bag, giving them a second task to perform before the end of the night. However, those who have had a goal from the start — to kill someone, etc. — must stick by their original goal as well as achieve this new one if they hope to win the game. If a player finds themselves with a note that tells them to kill someone who is already dead, they should be grateful, since their goal has already been achieved.

FLOOR CONFINEMENTS. After choosing a *Further Intentions* note, players have another 30 minutes to search the house and fulfill their tasks. However, this time they are each confined to a particular floor in order to keep away from any possible killers (dead players can go to any floor), and Floor cards are shuffled and distributed.

As host, you can also make suggestions on specific things players should look for during the second search, particularly involving clues that may give away whether or not the house is truly haunted. After 30 minutes, everyone returns to the living room for dessert and to conclude the game.

WINNING THE GAME. At the appointed hour, guests draw their conclusions as to whether or not the house is truly haunted or if it's all a hoax. If anyone has been killed, they should also discuss who the killer(s) may be.

After discussion, guests reveal all their secret notes and say whether or not they have fulfilled them. Checks are given to those who survived, adding in any money from those who died. Prizes are given to those who survived *and* accomplished their tasks, and those who died get to keep their noose. As the creator of the game, you should then reveal whether you set up the house to be haunted or a hoax, and how you did this.

Tips

- Remember that if you have less than 12 people at your gathering, remove the *Secret Notes* that refer to players with a number higher than your guest list. *Example: If you have a total of 9 players, remove any notes regarding Players 10, 11 and 12.*
- Although you already know whether the house is haunted, there are other things you can look for when searching rooms with the others. Look to see which player

takes what weapon, who searches rooms together or alone and the different ways players interpret their surroundings.

- Since this is a game involving murder, being sneaky is always allowed. Think up some ways to kill someone without ever being suspected, such as picking up a gun when others see you and then switching your weapon with a poison vial later.

- Add to the atmosphere by playing music from any of the three generations your story takes place in, such as classical music that Isabelle may have listened to, big band music that the Landrys may have listened to or modern music that your guests listen to today!

MAKE THIS GAME YOUR OWN!

Add your own flair to this murder mystery by writing a few of your own secret notes. You can also write a unique background story of what happened in the haunted house years ago, then set up different props and clues around your story.

LIKE THIS GAME?

Check out Mr. Grave's Gathering *in Chapter 7 for another murder mystery party in which players search the house for clues to uncover a killer among you!*

Invitation

Dear Friend,

I would like to invite you to a very special gathering on the night of _____.
I have rented the House on Haunted Hill, *and anyone who attends and is fortunate enough to survive until midnight will be rewarded a sum of $10,000.*

The story of the House on Haunted Hill is famous enough, as I'm sure you know. In case you are not familiar with it, however, the tale goes as follows:

In the late 1800s, a woman by the name of Isabelle Nightly resided in this house. It was rumored that she routinely performed black magic in the basement with the intention of conjuring demons and even summoning the Devil. No one ever suspected Isabelle of doing any real harm, and she eventually went insane and died in her bed at the age of 85. Years later, the bodies of four people were found scattered throughout the house, the dismembered parts and bones in almost all of the rooms. It is believed that these were poor souls that Isabelle used as sacrifices to the Devil.

Long after the remains were removed, the house stayed empty for many years until a young couple by the name of Landry bought it in 1948. Unaware of the history of the house, they moved in with their baby daughter. Two weeks later, Mrs. Landry suffered a terrible fall down the stairs and died instantly. The baby mysteriously disappeared soon after, and Mr. Landry went completely insane within days. He was put in a mental institution where he resided until dying in his sleep five years later at the age of 32.

The House on Haunted Hill is rumored to be haunted to this very day. I invite you to come and see if its legends are true — and of course, to win a most favorable prize for your bravery and morbid curiosity.

Until then,

Haunted House and Murder Mystery Party

Address: _____

Date: _____

Time: _____

(Please bring your camera!)

COPY @ 120%

Notes

SECRETS. • You're here to prove the house is haunted. If you find any items throughout the house that disappear later on, convince at least one other person that the place is really haunted.

- You're here to prove the haunting is a hoax. If you see any messages written around the house, erase them when no one is around. They were obviously written by a person and not a ghost.
- You've been promised $10,000 from a local newspaper if you get a picture of a ghost.
- If there are weapons in this place, you want the gun. Take it and keep it throughout the game.
- Try to scare another player to death to get their reward money. Take a few scary items from the house and put them directly in their path.
- You're convinced someone here is a killer. Make a point to see who takes what weapon throughout the house and write it in your notebook.
- You're here to bring Isabelle back from the dead. Find her secret spell in the house, but don't tell anyone you have it unless asked.
- You're afraid of ghosts but here for the money. If you see a ghost, hide behind another player until you leave the room.
- Pictures of the Devil terrify you. If there are any in the house, turn them so they face the wall.
- Use your camera and fake trying to get a picture of a ghost. Instead, try to get a picture of a *murder*.

DINNER NOTES. • Lie to the (living) player on your right about why you came to the House on Haunted Hill tonight.

- Lie to the (living) player on your left about why you came to the House on Haunted Hill tonight.
- Tell the (living) player on your right that you read in the paper the name of the Landry baby was Joshua.
- Tell the (living) player on your left that you heard Isabelle killed her victims by poisoning them with tainted cake.
- Ask the (living) player on your right if they have ever seen a ghost before tonight.
- Tell the (living) player on your left that almost a dozen people have snuck into this house over the years, but none have ever stayed more than 15 minutes.
- Tell the (living) player on your right that blood curdling screams can be heard from this house late at night.
- You are growing nervous about the (living) player on your left. Ask them if they have ever killed anyone.
- You are growing suspicious about the (living) player on your right. Ask them if they have a weapon.
- You are beginning to trust the (living) player on your left. Secretly tell them any suspicions you have of another player.

COPY @ 120%

- You are starting to dislike the (living) player on your right. Get a weapon and put it on their seat after everyone gets up from dinner.
- Ask the (living) player on your left about the most interesting thing they have seen in the house.

FURTHER INTENTIONS.

- This place is haunted and you know it. Prevent anyone from bringing Isabelle back from the dead at all costs, even if it means killing someone.
- This "haunted" story is a sham. Prove it by wearing the pendant cursed by the Devil.
- You realize a player of your choice is plotting something. Kill them.
- A player of your choice is trying to make others panic. Kill them before they start trouble.
- A player of your choice has been suspicious of you from the beginning. Mess with their head so they think you might kill them.
- If you discover any old, valuable items that belonged to anyone who lived in the House on Haunted Hill, steal them to sell later on.
- Try to convince a player of your choice that another player keeps switching weapons.
- A player of your choice is the only one you trust. Stay with them at all times for safety.
- Kill the next person you see take a weapon. That person is obviously a killer.
- Set the spirit of the Landry baby free: place the bible, crucifix and white candle in the middle of the ring of baby toys and light the candle.
- Refuse to be alone in any room — this place is haunted!

MURDER NOTES.

- Kill Player 1. He/she sent your brother to jail for life.
- Kill Player 2. You've always hated him/her.
- Kill Player 3. You think that he/she is out to kill off the guests for more reward money.
- Kill Player 4. You were paid to do this by an unknown source.
- Kill Player 5. You're almost sure that you saw him/her try to poison you.
- Kill Player 6. You want their share of the reward money.
- Kill Player 7. You want their share of the reward money.
- Kill Player 8. You think that she/he had an affair with your spouse.
- Kill Player 9. He/she's a jerk!
- Kill Player 10. He/she is so annoying.
- Kill Player 11. He/she gave you the evil eye.
- Kill Player 12. You're just dying to kill someone!

Isabelle's Secret Spell

To Bring the Dead Back to Life
Spell must be performed between 8–10 PM.

Light the black candle
Lighting thousands to their grave
Take the pendant from the dead
Now the Devil's slave
Place both within the circle
To finalize the spell
And say the cursed words:
Now return thee, back from hell!

Letter from the Antiques Dealer

October 1, 1885

Dear Ms. Nightly,

Enclosed you will find the exquisite gem necklace you ordered from my estab-lishment last month. I think you will find it to your satisfaction, as it is the one you have been begging me to unearth for years: the necklace rumored to have been touched by the Devil.

Please be warned that the jewelry is rumored to have extremely dangerous pow-ers. I would strongly advise against wearing it, but rather keep it in a safe place.

Thank you for your generous payment of $15,000.

Yours,

Roger Ellington

Frederick Loren
1 Ashton Place
New York, NY 10010

Date _____

Pay to the Order of: _____

Amount: _____ dollars

Memo: *I survived the* *House on Haunted Hill!!!*   Signature: _____

You must remain on the

First Floor

(However, you may *sneak* to other floors if you wish. If caught, make up a reason why you're there.)

You must remain on the

Second Floor

(However, you may *sneak* to other floors if you wish. If caught, make up a reason why you're there.)

You must remain on the

Basement Floor

(However, you may *sneak* to other floors if you wish. If caught, make up a reason why you're there.)

Host Sheet

Read (or paraphrase) the following at the beginning of the party:

"Welcome everyone to my party. My name is _____. You have all been invited to spend the evening at this house I have rented on Haunted Hill. There is a lot of history to this house: one of ghosts, witchcraft and murder. There is also a lot of money to be gained tonight. For each of you who survive until midnight, I will reward you a sum of $10,000. However, there are many dangers to be faced as well, as I am told the spirits who reside here do not take kindly to strangers. You may find that the souls of the dead are not the only things to be feared tonight. You see, for each of you who do not survive, the reward money will be split evenly between the remaining participants.

I invite you all to explore this House on Haunted Hill. Together we will decide for ourselves whether it is truly haunted, or only so in the imaginations of eager spectators. But tread lightly and take heed, both of the ghosts and ghouls among us, and each other.

Good luck to you all.

Explaining the Game

To begin, each of you will be assigned a particular number. You will retain your real name throughout the evening, but your number will help you better identify each other in the game. (Shuffle the number tags and distribute them.)

*Next, each of you will choose one note from this bag. Don't show your note to **anyone**. Whatever your note instructs you to do, you must fulfill it before midnight if you hope to win the game. There are all kinds of notes here, some instructing you to discover secrets of the house, others to trust or distrust a fellow player, and others to kill them.* (Everyone takes a note.)

Throughout your wanderings, you will come across various weapons in the house. Weapons consist of guns, knives, poison vials, nooses and "Chandelier Falls" cards. If you choose to take a weapon, you may take only one at a time. Or, if you choose to use the weapon right then and there, you may do that, too. However, you should not hide weapons in the house.

*If you do have the intention of killing someone, this is done by showing your weapon to that player in **secret** when no one else is around. Players who are killed should not scream or make any sign of a struggle to attract attention. If you are killed, you must quietly put any weapons or other game items on the floor where you were killed. You must then take a noose from the wall, write on it how you died, and wear it throughout the rest of the evening. Dead players are allowed to speak, but cannot speak about anything relating to the game, including revealing who killed them.*

It is important to note that you do not want to get caught killing someone, because if you do, whoever catches you has every right to kill you without being penalized for it. Anyone who kills a player without reason is disqualified and receives no money or prizes.

At any time you may ask another player what their intentions are for the night. But of course, everyone is permitted to lie.

*In order to win the game, you must survive until midnight **and** perform any and all actions on your chosen note.*

COPY @ 120%

Host Sheet

Playing the Game

1. SEARCHING THE HOUSE. Once notes have been chosen and everyone understands the rules of play, suggest everyone split up and search the house to look for any signs of ghosts. You will go on the search, as well, since you are not familiar with the house and have only rented it for the evening. (If you have shut doors to any rooms that are not part of the game, tell this to the guests.) Players may either search by themselves or with others — if they trust them. Encourage everyone to take a notebook for writing down any clues they come across. Everyone should return to the living room in 30 minutes, at which time they will discuss their findings before sitting down to dinner. Mention that there is no need to rush through the house, as they will have additional time to explore later.

2. CLUE DISCUSSION. After the search, ask players to discuss any clues they came across, and if they have any reason to believe the house is haunted. If anyone has been killed at this point, players should also discuss who may be the killer. After discussion, invite everyone to sit down for dinner.

3. DINNER. When everyone sits down to dinner, pass around the purple bag and have each player choose a dinner note. In addition to discussing the topics on their notes, encourage players to talk about why they have chosen to spend the night on Haunted Hill. For example, was it to find evidence of ghosts, or merely for the money? Ask what they will do with their $10,000, and what they would do with more money if the sum were to be increased due to untimely deaths. Casually mention that anyone who has the poison could kill someone during dinner, if they show them their poison vial in secret.

4. FURTHER INTENTIONS. After dinner, ask the players if anyone has found any written clues from either Isabelle's or the Landrys' time. If either piece of writing has been uncovered, the player should read it aloud, as others may wish to use it to their advantage. Note that if any players wish to perform the spell, they must wait until the appointed hour.

Next, have each player choose a *Further Intentions* note from the red bag. Inform them that these are the final instructions they will get for the night, and they must fulfill what is listed on **all** notes if they hope to win the game. If any player's *Further Intentions* note contradicts their Secret Clues note, they must discard it and pick again.

5. FLOOR SEARCH. Once the new notes have been chosen and any further clues discussed, instruct the guests to split up once again, specifically to look for anything in the house they heard about from other players and to fulfill their secret notes. Pose specific questions they should try and solve in their search, such as:

Is the ghost of Isabelle in the house?
Have all 4 of Isabelle's sacrifices been found?
Are the ghosts of the Landrys still here?
Are there any signs of what happened to the Landry baby?

However, due to possible distrust and fear of killers among them, this second search will be confined to a particular floor of the house. Shuffle and distribute the Floor cards so that each player has an assigned floor. (Dead players may go anywhere.) If players absolutely refuse to go to the floor on their card, they may trade cards with another player. Tell everyone to be alert during their search — especially if someone has been killed! — and return in 30 minutes to the living room for dessert and reward money.

6. MIDNIGHT. Just before midnight (or the appointed hour), dessert is served. Afterwards, guests should each draw conclusions as to whether or not the house is truly haunted or if it's all a hoax. If anyone has been killed, they should also discuss who the killer(s) must be. After discussion, guests reveal all their notes and say whether or not they have fulfilled them.

Those who survived but did not fulfill their notes get a check of $10,000, adding in any extra money from those who died. Those who survived and did fulfill their notes get a check and prize. However, if a player was caught killing someone but was not killed as a result, they do not get the check but do get their prize. (Killers who were not caught but only accused get the check and prize.) Those who died get to keep their nooses.

As host, reveal whether you set up the house to be haunted or a hoax.

COPY @ 120%

SECTION II
DARK COMEDIES

Monster movies have always contained humor in one way or another. Whether it's a severed head rolling down the alley or a town dope quivering before an alien ray gun, there's always a quick moment to laugh before our inevitable demise.

Dark comedies reverse the scenario and make most everything funny while the slayings and invasions occur during odd intervals. Heroes usually reflect how the average person would handle an everyday situation that suddenly goes way too far, like concealing a triple homicide in the parlor or battling a Stay Puft Marshmallow Man with a proton pack.

The films in this section are some of the best dark comedies to hit the screen, and the games they inspire allow you to take on the roles of some of your favorite sneaky and shady characters, as well as make up new ones from your own demented mind. Large group games bring players into a murder mystery in which accusations fly and stage a dance party in a torture chamber, while others test your business skills as paranormal eliminators and teach you to cast deadly spells as specialized witches and warlocks.

For years you've embraced your favorite dark comedies to recite the punch lines and escape into their most bizarre realities. Now you can enter the worlds you know so well and make them your own with witchcraft, hauntings and a few mass murders along the way.

6

GHOSTBUSTERS: ON THE CASE

Ghostbusting and Trivia Game
based on *Ghostbusters (1984)*,
4–8 players

Has anyone seen the movie *Ghostbusters* and *not* wanted to become a paranormal investigator, armed with a proton pack and ghost trap? Of course not. And that's what we love about it: the bizarre and far-fetched view of the paranormal, with ghosts flying left and right and people getting slimed everywhere.

But what would being a paranormal eliminator *really* involve? When ghosts run amok and the professionals are called into action, would cash rain from the sky like blown-up marshmallow, or would each case be up to chance when dealing with destructive demons, city officials and the fate of the world on your shoulders?

THE GAME

In this game of ghosts and business practice, players get to see what ghostbusting is really about: being knowledgeable about the world of the paranormal, properly assessing the nature of hauntings and trying to make a living through paranormal eliminating. Teams aim to earn as much money as they can in their ghostly trade while avoiding bankruptcy and the sketchy doings of ghosts and humans alike. You will need:

- 2 Blank Dice • Sheet of Ghost and Skull Stickers • Black Paint
- Fine Paint Brush • Pen **for each Team**

PREPARING THE GAME

To create *Ghostbusters: On the Case*, you'll need to put together the following: Paranormal Study Sheets, Ghostbusters Cases, and Ghostbusters Dice.

PARANORMAL STUDY SHEETS. Photocopy the Paranormal Studies sheets below and send one set to each player **a week before playing the game**. This sheet includes information that real ghost hunters study for their line of work and will be used as trivia in the game. However, players will not to able to use their sheets *during* the game.

GHOSTBUSTERS CASES. Next, photocopy the 16 Ghostbusters cases, each of which includes trivia, haunting activity and a special scenario. You'll also find a sample case to see how the cases will be filled in and a blank case for making new cases in future games.

DICE. Lastly, make a pair of Ghostbusters dice to use for busting ghosts. Place 2 ghost stickers and 2 skull stickers on a pair of blank dice, and paint a black X on the 2 remaining sides.

PLAYING THE GAME

To play the game, put the Ghostbusters Cases face down on the game table and split the players into teams of 2 or 3. Each team will want to make as much money as they can as paranormal investigators and eliminators by answering trivia on paranormal studies, properly assessing hauntings and busting ghosts.

TRIVIA. Each turn, a team chooses a Ghostbusters case and immediately gives it to **another** team for quizzing them on the trivia and case assessment. Each team member can only answer 1 trivia question per case. For each question answered correctly, the team gets $1,000. For each trivia question that is not a True or False question and is answered incorrectly, a player on another team may guess for $500. The team with the least amount of money is given the option to do this. Players should keep a running total of their wages on the bottom of their cases to know who is making the most/least money throughout the game.

CASE ASSESSMENTS. After the trivia has been answered, the team is then read the haunting activity so that they can properly assess the case as one of a ghost, spirit, demon or poltergeist. (Descriptions of each are listed on the Paranormal Studies sheets.) Correct assessments earn $500, but incorrect assessments **cannot** be answered by another team. The team is then given their case for busting the ghost.

BUSTING GHOSTS. To bust the ghost, players roll the dice once. The following rolls determine the outcome of the bust:

- *2 Ghosts:* Ghost destroys the place and gets away.
- *2 X:* Ghost is busted!
- *2 Skulls:* Bankrupt! Lose all your money earned to this point. No bills need payment this turn. (2 Skulls have no effect on second attempts at cases.)
- *1 Ghost and 1 Skull:* No bust.
- *1 X and 1 Ghost:* Busted!
- *1 X and 1 Skull:* Ghost runs, then busted!

Successful busts pay $5,000 unless the case has a special scenario that affects the wage. Any unresolved case in which the ghost gets away remains on the table to be tried again **in addition** to taking a new case. If the original case was not properly assessed, this can also be tried for the full $500. After the bust, the team adds up their total wage for the trivia, assessment and ghost bust. A sum of $1,000 is subtracted from each case for bills, food and equipment.

WINNING THE GAME. Once all the cases have been gone through **once**, the team with the most money wins.

MAKE THIS GAME YOUR OWN!

After you've played this game, you can make additional games with the blank Ghostbusters case. Photocopy 16–20 blank cases and allow each player to fill out 2–3 before the game begins. Players can write trivia based on their knowledge of the world of the paranormal, well-documented hauntings, trivia from the film Ghostbusters *or questions on other films about ghosts. Players can also write each haunting activity, case assessment and special scenario. They should then write their initials on the back of each case so they know not to choose their own cases in the game.*

Ghostbusters: On the Case

Object of the Game

Earn as much money as you can
as paranormal investigators and eliminators.

Players split into teams of 2 or 3. Ghostbusters cases are put face down on the game table with the set of dice. Each turn, a team chooses one case. Another team takes it to quiz them on trivia and case assessment.

TRIVIA. Each player on a team can only answer 1 trivia question per case. **Trivia questions earn $1,000 each.** Any trivia question that is not a True or False question and is answered incorrectly may be tried by another team for $500. Teams with the **least** amount of money are given the option to do this first.

CASE ASSESSMENTS. The team is read the haunting activity for their case and must properly assess the haunting as a demon, poltergeist, spirit or ghost. **Correct case assessments earn $500.** (If answered incorrectly, other teams may **not** try to assess the case.)

BUSTING GHOSTS. The team rolls the dice once to try and bust the ghost:
- *2 Ghosts:* Ghost destroys the place and gets away.
- *2 X:* Ghost is busted!
- *2 Skulls:* Bankrupt! Lose all your money earned to this point. No bills need payment this turn. (2 Skulls have no effect on second attempts at cases.)
- *1 Ghost and 1 Skull:* No bust.
- *1 X and 1 Ghost:* Busted!
- *1 X and 1 Skull:* Ghost runs, then busted!

A successful bust earns $5,000 unless stated otherwise in the Special Scenario. If a case does not end in a bust, it remains in the game for any team to try again on a future turn **in addition** to taking a new case. If the original case was not properly assessed, this can also be tried for the full $500.

WINNING THE GAME. Once all the cases have been gone through **once**, the team with the most money wins.

Paranormal Studies: Ghostbusters Training Prerequisite

GHOSTS AND OTHER SUPERNATURAL ENTITIES. According to the guide *How to be a Ghost Hunter*, the difference between a spirit and a ghost is that a ghost is the **residual energy** of a person or psychic recording of a person after death, while a spirit is the **sentient presence** of an individual who has remained in the material world after death. Ghosts may be partially visible or fully visible. **Apparitions** are fully visible ghosts, and are sometimes referred to as **phantasms**. Ghosts that appear only briefly in a viewer's peripheral vision are known as **shadow people.**

A **living ghost** can be 1 of 2 phenomena:

1. Someone who dies and makes a psychic connection with a friend or family member at the moment of death, or

2. Someone who is still alive, in need of aid or suffering in some way and makes a psychic connection to get help.

A **poltergeist** is typically caused by the mental energy of an individual or family experiencing severe psychological tensions. Poltergeist is German for "**noisy ghost.**" This type of entity generally requires counseling for the human agent involved.

A haunting involving a **demon** requires an exorcism or blessing.

The immaterial substance believed to be the transparent, corporeal presence of a spirit or ghost is known as **ectoplasm**. Ectoplasm is visible as **vapors and mists.**

STUDIES AND PRACTICES. Paranormal phenomenon is known to cause the surrounding air to **ionize**. Ionization meters and Electromagnetic Field Meters (**EMF meters**) are commonly used in paranormal investigations. **EEG meters**, which record the electrical activity in the brain, are typically not used.

Electronic Voice Phenomenon (EVP) refers to inaudible sounds that are detected on electronic recording media and are believed to be caused by spirits.

The word "**parapsychology**" was started in the 1930s to separate the studies of ESP and psychokinesis from ghost investigations.

The Society for Paranormal Research, also known as SPR, was formed in 1882 and is located in Great Britain.

A **séance** is a meeting in which a spiritualist attempts to communicate with the spirits of the dead. Objects that appear out of thin air during a séance or paranormal investigation are called **apports.**

Past-life regression involves the re-experiencing of living in the past with a different body and personality.

Literally translated, "**occult**" means "knowledge of the hidden" in Latin.

PSYCHIC PHENOMENON. **Telepathy** refers to a person acquiring information from another person's mind.

Clairvoyance refers to seeing information about a place, event or object without naturally viewing it.

ESP, or extra sensory perception, refers to the perception of communication outside of normal sensory capabilities, and includes telepathy and clairvoyance. **A deck of playing cards** is often used to test for ESP abilities.

Precognition is the experience of seeing information about a future event.

Intuitions refer to ordinary psychological processes at the unconscious level.

An **Out of Body experience**, or OBE, typically involves a sensation of levitation and in some cases perceiving one's own body while outside of it. It is possible to induce these experiences deliberately through visualization while in a relaxed, meditative state. This is also referred to as **astral projection**.

A **Near Death Experience**, or NDE, is a personal experience that encompasses a sensation of levitation and being detached from the body, an ambiance of security and warmth, and the presence of an all-loving being of light, sometimes interpreted as God. Cases are reported after being pronounced clinically dead or very close to death.

Psychokinesis is the ability to affect objects, events or people around you without physical contact. Psychokinesis literally translates to "**soul motion**" or "**mind motion**."

A **medium** is someone who can communicate between the natural and spirit worlds.

Channeling refers to receiving messages or inspiration from spirits.

Possession refers to a malevolent entity gaining control over a person's body and possessing it until forced to leave through an exorcism.

The first documented report of **paranormal photography** came from William Mumler in Britain in 1862.

An **aura** is the presence of an energy field around our bodies.

QUICK REFERENCE FOR ASSESSING HAUNTING ACTIVITY. **Demon**: An evil presence that

may cause bad odors, religious statues to be broken or moved, walls to bleed or human possession.

Poltergeist: A presence that may cause items to be moved, thrown or misplaced throughout the house, lights to flicker and tables or beds to shake.

Ghost: An entity that does not recognize the presence of people, but rather reenacts a certain period from their life.

Spirit: An entity that is not evil in nature and recognizes people around it, interacts with them or tries to make contact.

Sample Case: Ghostbusters Case

TRIVIA. 1. What type of supernatural entity requires an exorcism or blessing? *A demon*

2. What is a meeting in which a spiritualist attempts to communicate with the spirits of the dead? *A séance*

ACTIVITY. Location: *Large, old house in Amityville, New York*

Situation: *Unnatural presence felt in the basement, walls bleeding, husband possessed, voices heard.*

Any Tangible Presence Sighted: *No.*

Situation Witnessed By: *Mother and kids.*

Case Assessment: Demon

Special Scenario: Roll any skulls and the demon escapes.

WAGES

Trivia ($1,000 each)	$2,000
Case Assessment ($500)	$500
Ghost Bust	$5,000
Total Income (Minus $1,000 Expenses)	$6,500

Income from Additional Trivia _____ *Running Total* _____

Ghostbusters Case

TRIVIA. 1. What type of supernatural entity requires an exorcism or blessing? *A demon*

2. What is a meeting in which a spiritualist attempts to communicate with the spirits of the dead? *A séance*

ACTIVITY. Location: *Gettysburg battlefield.*

Situation: *Apparitions of soldiers running across field late at night, then falling down as if struck or shot. No contact made with people around.*

Any Tangible Presence Sighted: *Yes.*

Situation Witnessed By: *Tourists to Gettysburg.*

Case Assessment: Ghost

Special Scenario: Roll any skulls and this one escapes.

WAGES

Trivia ($1,000 each)	_____
Case Assessment ($500)	_____
Ghost Bust	_____
Total Income (Minus $1,000 Expenses)	_____

Income from Additional Trivia _____ *Running Total* _____

Ghostbusters Case

TRIVIA. 1. According to *How to be a Ghost Hunter*, there is a difference between a spirit and a ghost. Which is known as the **sentient presence** of an individual who has remained in the material world after death? *A spirit*

2. True or False: EEG meters are typically used more often than EMF meters during paranormal field investigations. *False*

ACTIVITY. Location: *Maryland.*
Situation: *Apparition of a teenage boy with a large head wound. Tries to communicate to home owners to help him escape his stepfather.*
Any Tangible Presence Sighted: *Yes.*
Situation Witnessed By: *Home owners.*

Case Assessment: Spirit.

Special Scenario: This spirit isn't too bright. Roll any skulls and it's busted.

WAGES
Trivia ($1,000 each)   _____
Case Assessment ($500)   _____
Ghost Bust   _____
Total Income (Minus $1,000 Expenses)   _____
Income from Additional Trivia _____   *Running Total* _____

Ghostbusters Case

TRIVIA. 1. What type of phenomenon is typically caused by the mental energy of an individual or family experiencing severe psychological tensions? An apparition, **a poltergeist**, a demon

2. True or False: ESP refers to the perception of communication outside of normal sensory capabilities, including telepathy and clairvoyance. *True*

ACTIVITY. Location: *Small town in Ohio.*
Situation: *Figure appearing in the middle of the night in the hallway and bedrooms. Dark vapor takes on the form of a man in mid–30s with red eyes and a bad odor.*
Any Tangible Presence Sighted: *Yes.*
Situation Witnessed By: *Husband, wife and kids.*

Case Assessment: Demon.

Special Scenario: Client can't afford to pay the total wage. They pay $3,000 and give cookies.

WAGES
Trivia ($1,000 each)   _____
Case Assessment ($500)   _____
Ghost Bust   _____
Total Income (Minus $1,000 Expenses)   _____
Income from Additional Trivia _____   *Running Total* _____

COPY @ 120%

Ghostbusters Case

TRIVIA. 1. True or False: A malevolent entity gaining control over a person's body until forced to leave through an exorcism is referred to as "possession." *True*

2. What society located in Great Britain and formed in 1882 is referred to as SPR? *The Society for Paranormal Research*

ACTIVITY. Location: *Rural Maine.*

Situation: *House with objects being repeatedly thrown throughout the kitchen and living room, windows and doors slamming open and shut at odd times throughout the night.*

Any Tangible Presence Sighted: *No.*

Situation Witnessed By: *Home owners and neighbors.*

Case Assessment: Poltergeist.

Special Scenario: Get this one and end up on TV. Get an extra $1,000.

WAGES

Trivia ($1,000 each)
Case Assessment ($500)
Ghost Bust
Total Income (Minus $1,000 Expenses)
Income from Additional Trivia _____   *Running Total* _____

Ghostbusters Case

TRIVIA. 1. Inaudible sounds that are detected on electronic recording media and are believed to be spirits are known as what? *Electronic Voice Phenomenon (EVP)*

2. Astral Projection is another term for which: Out of Body Experience or Near Death Experience? *Out of Body Experience*

ACTIVITY. Location: *Colorado Springs Hotel.*

Situation: *Image of a woman jumping off the hotel balcony. Happens nightly at 2:10 AM.*

Any Tangible Presence Sighted: *Yes.*

Situation Witnessed By: *Hotel guests and management.*

Case Assessment: Ghost

Special Scenario: Break anything (roll 1 ghost) and clients only pay you half your wage.

WAGES

Trivia ($1,000 each)
Case Assessment ($500)
Ghost Bust
Total Income (Minus $1,000 Expenses)
Income from Additional Trivia _____   *Running Total* _____

COPY @ 120%

Ghostbusters Case

TRIVIA. 1. The word "parapsychology" was started in the 1930s to separate studies of which 2 unusual mental abilities from ghost investigations? **ESP and psychokinesis**, poltergeist phenomenon and spiritual photography, fire starting and levitation

2. True or False: Telepathy is referred to as the experience of seeing information about a future event. *False (Precognition)*

ACTIVITY. Location: *Michigan.*

Situation: *Figure of a man dressed in a dark suit. Appears outside during the hours of 11 AM and 2 PM. Pushes children on the swings, plays tea party and tells stories that took place over a hundred years ago.*

Any Tangible Presence Sighted: *Yes.*

Situation Witnessed By: *6 year-old boy.*

Case Assessment: Spirit.

Special Scenario: Don't break anything (roll no ghosts) and clients give an extra $1,000.

WAGES

Trivia ($1,000 each)   _____

Case Assessment ($500)   _____

Ghost Bust   _____

Total Income (Minus $1,000 Expenses)   _____

Income from Additional Trivia _____   *Running Total* _____

Ghostbusters Case

TRIVIA. 1. What type of paranormal entity is generally stopped after the human agent involved has attended counseling? Demon; **Poltergeist**; Slimer

2. True or False: Ectoplasm is seen in forms of vapors and mists. *True*

ACTIVITY. Location: *Rural community, North Dakota.*

Situation: *Teenager afflicted by unknown disease or condition. Symptoms include face distortion, violent outbursts and speaking with an unnatural-sounding voice. Unknown scars formed on upper body.*

Any Tangible Presence Sighted: *No.*

Situation Witnessed By: *Parents and neighbors.*

Case Assessment: Demon.

Special Scenario: Screw up and you're sued. (Lose $5,000)

WAGES

Trivia ($1,000 each)   _____

Case Assessment ($500)   _____

Ghost Bust   _____

Total Income (Minus $1,000 Expenses)   _____

Income from Additional Trivia _____   *Running Total* _____

COPY @ 120%

Ghostbusters Case

TRIVIA. 1. The word "poltergeist" is German for what?
Noisy ghost

2. A fully visible ghost is referred to as what? Shadow people, **an apparition**, Stay Puft Marshmallow Man

ACTIVITY. Location: *Small Connecticut town.*

Situation: *Furniture and items in upstairs bedroom continually flying through the air in a circle.*

Any Tangible Presence Sighted: *No.*

Situation Witnessed By: *Home owners.*

Case Assessment: Poltergeist

Special Scenario: **This client thinks you're cute. Get an extra roll.**

WAGES

Trivia ($1,000 each)
Case Assessment ($500)   _____
Ghost Bust   _____
Total Income (Minus $1,000 Expenses)   _____
Income from Additional Trivia _____   *Running Total* _____

Ghostbusters Case

TRIVIA. 1. What phenomenon is referred to as NDE?
Near Death Experience

2. True or False: Intuitions are a type of paranormal phenomena in which one sees information about a place, event or object without naturally viewing it?
False (Clairvoyance)

ACTIVITY. Location: *Victorian Cemetery, Upper Massachusetts.*

Situation: *Woman dressed in an 18th century–style gown walking out the front gate and across the road, waving to no one in sight.*

Any Tangible Presence Sighted: *Yes.*

Situation Witnessed By: *People driving by.*

Case Assessment: Ghost.

Special Scenario: **If you roll two ghosts, they also break your equipment. (Lose $1,000)**

WAGES

Trivia ($1,000 each)
Case Assessment ($500)   _____
Ghost Bust   _____
Total Income (Minus $1,000 Expenses)   _____
Income from Additional Trivia _____   *Running Total* _____

COPY @ 120%

Ghostbusters Case

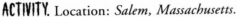

TRIVIA. 1. True or False: *Psychokinesis* is the ability to affect objects, events or people around you without physical contact. *True*

2. A deck of playing cards are often used to test for what abilities? Intuitions, insanity, **ESP**

ACTIVITY. Location: *Salem, Massachusetts.*

Situation: *The feeling of a small child tugging dresses and coats of young women near cemetery gates. Happens between 9 PM and midnight.*

Any Tangible Presence Sighted: *No.*

Situation Witnessed By: *Several tourists.*

Case Assessment: Spirit

Special Scenario: Mess this one up and the State gets on your back. Lose $1,000 dealing with them.

WAGES
Trivia ($1,000 each) _____
Case Assessment ($500) _____
Ghost Bust _____
Total Income (Minus $1,000 Expenses) _____
Income from Additional Trivia _____   *Running Total* _____

Ghostbusters Case

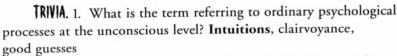

TRIVIA. 1. What is the term referring to ordinary psychological processes at the unconscious level? **Intuitions**, clairvoyance, good guesses

2. What phenomenon is referred to as OBE? *Out of Body experience*

ACTIVITY. Location: *Northern Florida.*

Situation: *Young couple hearing voices throughout their new home. Cold spots throughout the house, religious objects being moved and broken, husband found claw marks on his ankles, wife pushed down the stairs when she was alone.*

Any Tangible Presence Sighted: *No.*

Situation Witnessed By: *Home owners.*

Case Assessment: Demon

Special Scenario: This client's rich. Get an extra $2,000 if you catch the demon.

WAGES
Trivia ($1,000 each) _____
Case Assessment ($500) _____
Ghost Bust _____
Total Income (Minus $1,000 Expenses) _____
Income from Additional Trivia _____   *Running Total* _____

COPY @ 120%

Ghostbusters Case

TRIVIA. 1. What is the presence of an energy field around our bodies? *An aura*

2. True or False: If someone is still alive, in need of aid or suffering in some way and makes a psychic connection to get help, their spirit is referred to as a living ghost. *True*

ACTIVITY. Location: *Wisconsin apartment.*

Situation: *Items constantly misplaced in a woman's home, who lives alone. Objects seen flying through the air, including kitchen knives and small tools.*

Any Tangible Presence Sighted: *No.*

Situation Witnessed By: *Apartment renter.*

Case Assessment: Poltergeist.

Special Scenario: You got lost trying to find the place. Only a roll of 2 X's will stop the poltergeist now.

WAGES
Trivia ($1,000 each)   _____
Case Assessment ($500)   _____
Ghost Bust   _____
Total Income (Minus $1,000 Expenses)   _____
Income from Additional Trivia _____   *Running Total* _____

Ghostbusters Case

TRIVIA. 1. "Psychokinesis" literally translates to what? Movement without contact, **soul motion**, weirdo

2. The first documented report of paranormal photography came from William Mumler in Britain in what year? 1845, **1862**, 2002

ACTIVITY. Location: *Second hand shop in Nebraska.*

Situation: *Foul smell in the attic, appearance of blood seen on the walls on 1st and 2nd floor. Customers suddenly develop sad or mad dispositions when entering the shop.*

Any Tangible Presence Sighted: *No.*

Situation Witnessed By: *Store owner and customers.*

Case Assessment: Demon

Special Scenario: This demon is a prankster. Roll any skulls (including bankruptcy) and you catch it.

WAGES
Trivia ($1,000 each)   _____
Case Assessment ($500)   _____
Ghost Bust   _____
Total Income (Minus $1,000 Expenses)   _____
Income from Additional Trivia _____   *Running Total* _____

Ghostbusters Case

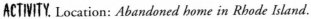

TRIVIA. 1. What is a person called who claims to be able to communicate between the natural and spirit worlds? *A medium*

2. True or False: Ghosts that appear only briefly in a viewer's peripheral vision are called apparitions. *False (Shadow people)*

ACTIVITY. Location: *Abandoned home in Rhode Island.*

Situation: *Figure seen floating among the trees after midnight, always walking down towards the lake.*

Any Tangible Presence Sighted: *Yes.*

Situation Witnessed By: *People driving by.*

Case Assessment: Ghost.

Special Scenario: **This ghost is so big it barely fits in the trap. Only a roll of 2 X's can get it.**

WAGES

Trivia ($1,000 each)   _____
Case Assessment ($500)   _____
Ghost Bust   _____
Total Income (Minus $1,000 Expenses)   _____
Income from Additional Trivia _____   *Running Total* _____

Ghostbusters Case

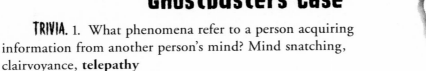

TRIVIA. 1. What phenomena refer to a person acquiring information from another person's mind? Mind snatching, clairvoyance, **telepathy**

2. True or False: Paranormal phenomenon is known to cause the surrounding air to ionize. *True*

ACTIVITY. Location: *Town Library, Kentucky.*

Situation: *Appearance of a white fog floating in the archives, known to follow workers on several occasions. Cold areas felt in the lower levels.*

Any Tangible Presence Sighted: *Yes.*

Situation Witnessed By: *Librarians and volunteers.*

Case Assessment: Spirit

Special Scenario: **This spirit gets angry when fired upon. Roll any ghosts and lose $1,000 in hospital bills.**

WAGES

Trivia ($1,000 each)   _____
Case Assessment ($500)   _____
Ghost Bust   _____
Total Income (Minus $1,000 Expenses)   _____
Income from Additional Trivia _____   *Running Total* _____

COPY @ 120%

Ghostbusters Case

TRIVIA. 1. Which has been known to be deliberately induced through visualization while in a meditative state: Out of Body Experiences or Near Death Experiences? *Out of Body Experiences*

2. Objects that appear out of thin air during a séance or paranormal investigation are referred to as what? Icons, **apports**, gifts

ACTIVITY. Location: *Office Building, Upstate New York.*

Situation: *Papers thrown off shelves and copiers when no one is around, storage boxes thrown down hallways. People pushed down escalators when no one is behind them.*

Any Tangible Presence Sighted: *No.*

Situation Witnessed By: *Office Workers.*

Case Assessment: Poltergeist

Special Scenario: This one is tricky. Roll any skulls and you lose the case.

WAGES

Trivia ($1,000 each)   _____
Case Assessment ($500)   _____
Ghost Bust   _____
Total Income (Minus $1,000 Expenses)   _____
Income from Additional Trivia _____   *Running Total* _____

Ghostbusters Case

TRIVIA.

ACTIVITY.

Location:
Situation:
Any Tangible Presence Sighted:
Situation Witnessed By:

Case Assessment:

Special Scenario:

WAGES

Trivia ($1,000 each)   _____
Case Assessment ($500)   _____
Ghost Bust   _____
Total Income (Minus $1,000 Expenses)   _____
Income from Additional Trivia _____   *Running Total* _____

7

MR. GRAVE'S GATHERING

Murder Mystery Game
based on *Clue (1985)*,
8 players

Imagine yourself caught in the middle of a murder. One dark and stormy evening you're called to a house full of strangers — none of whom are willing to reveal anything about themselves, not even their own name — when suddenly someone turns up dead. What would you do? Who could you trust? Anyone could be the killer, and everyone is hiding a dark secret ... just like you.

Such is the case in *Clue*, one our favorite board games brought to life. The six infamous characters now reveal unique personalities and backgrounds, each mysterious and hilarious in their own way. But what about the new characters introduced? What about the Cook, Yvette, Mr. Boddy, the Cop, the Motorist and the Telegram Girl? How did they end up there? What's their deal? In this murder mystery game, these sly strangers get caught up in a murderous scenario all their own.

THE GAME

In this murder mystery party, guests play the roles of the lesser-known characters in the film *Clue*. This story, however, takes place in 1947, seven years *before* the movie is set. Each player is given a pseudonym as well as all the information about their role beforehand. And since little is revealed about these characters in the film, players can actually shape their roles into almost anything they like.

As host, you take on the role of a character that is *not* in the film: an employee of the late host named Roxy (or Ox for a male role). You'll have the biggest role in the game which involves creating a mysterious atmosphere and moving events along from one scene to the next. You will need:

Murder Weapons: • Pipe • Dagger • Wrench • Rope • Wire
• Candlestick • Poison • Small Saw • Switchblade • Sledgehammer
• Worker's Gloves • Screwdriver • Kitchen Knife • Knife Sharpener
Props & Clues: • 12–15 3 × 5" Plain Index Cards • 8 Long Straws
• 8 Small Notebooks and Pens • 7 8 × 10" Boxes wrapped in Purple Ribbon
• Manilla Envelope • White Envelope
• Stuffed Dummy (wearing a Man's Suit and Hat) • Fake Gun
• Fake Blood • Wine Decanter • Wine Glass • Strip of Jean Fabric
• Assortment of Colored Feathers • Assortment of Colored Buttons
• Scissors • Small Black Gift Bag • Double-Sided Tape

STORY OF THE GAME

Seven people in Washington are hiding a secret, each involving murder or other sinister crimes. Mr. Grave, an eccentric millionaire possessing a well-known collection of serial killer weapons, has invited them all to his home for a small party. To keep their identities hidden, he has assigned them each a pseudonym. His intentions, however, are not of a friendly social but of blackmail, which his guests do not realize ... except for one.

Before the party begins, one guest arrives early and kills Mr. Grave, knowing fully well what he is up to. Mr. Grave's body is discovered at the beginning of the party by Roxy, an employee of the now dead host. Completely shocked, Roxy and the guests decide not to leave the mansion until they figure out who killed Mr. Grave, as everyone has reason to be accused and falsely charged due to their questionable backgrounds.

To make matters more complicated, a number of weapons are found in the parlor, each originally wrapped in a gift box and apparently for the guests. Some of them have been opened while others don't look touched, but one of the weapons was used to kill Mr. Grave.

The night becomes one of searching the entire house for clues and making gross accusations as the guests try to uncover who the killer is, where the crime was done, and with what weapon.

PREPARING THE GAME

To create your murder mystery game, you'll need to do the following:
- Assign players to character roles
- Set up the house murder-mystery style
- Assemble clues and murder weapons
- Assemble serial killer weapons and labels
- Prepare Room cards, Place cards, straws and notebooks
- Seal the story of *What Really Happened*

CHARACTERS. To assign players to specific roles, choose 7 people you want to invite to the party: 4 men and 3 women. Photocopy the Invitations and Character Biographies below to mail to the guests at least **one week** before the party. Each player should only be sent their *own* Character Biography. *(Note: If you don't want to know the outcome of the story, don't read the Character Biographies past the first paragraph!)* You may want to assign roles based on age, personality, or just the type of character you think each guest would have the most fun portraying.

Next, photocopy the Game Sheets to give to each player *at* the party, including the Roxy/Ox sheet for yourself. Feel free to read this sheet before the night of the party to get a sense of how the game will go.

SET UP. Use any number of rooms in your house for setting up the props and murderous décor, keeping the doors to any rooms you do not want used in the game shut. Deck out the place the way that Mr. Grave would: light a fire in the fireplace, hang large portraits (from your local thrift store) in the parlor and arrange a tray of a liquors and glasses.

Next, set up the following clues for players to discover as they search the house. You may wish to alter the list to reflect different areas of the house that you use in the game.

Front Yard   • 2 dog chains tied around a tree or pole

Hallway   • A drop of blood on the wall

Stairs   • A strip of jean cloth on a stair

Bedroom   • A wine decanter and half-filled glass of wine on the dresser
- A blackmail letter on the nightstand (discussed below)

Kitchen   • Dirty footprints by the back door

Bathroom   • A box of different colored buttons and feathers in the medicine cabinet
- A strand of rope on the floor

Parlor   • A lamp on the floor

- A dead body (stuffed dummy wearing suit and hat with a fake gun in his pocket) in the closet
- 7 wrapped murder weapons on a coffee table (discussed below)
- 8 small notebooks and pens on an end table

Spare Room • An open window (the only open window in the house)
- Collection of labeled serial killer weapons (discussed below)

CLUES AND MURDER WEAPONS.
Photocopy the *Clues for the Big Envelope* below, then cut out each paragraph and place in a manilla envelope marked "Roxy" (or "Ox"). Put the envelope on a desk or coffee table in the parlor.

Next, photocopy or hand-write the Blackmailing Letter below. Paperclip a small piece of paper to the letter which reads: *"Mr. Grave—Sorry, I opened your letter by accident.— Roxy. (or Ox)"* Plant the letter in Mr. Grave's bedroom.

To assemble the gift-wrapped weapons, put each of the following in a 10 × 8 × 5" box. Tie the boxes with purple ribbon and place them on the coffee table in the parlor. You'll see that some of the boxes should be re-opened after you tie them, while others should remain tied.

- Pipe: Ribbon untied, trace of blood on weapon
- Dagger: Ribbon untied, bloody fingerprint on weapon
- Wrench: Ribbon tied   • Rope: Ribbon untied   • Candlestick: Ribbon tied
- Wire: Ribbon tied   • Poison Vial: Ribbon untied, trace of blood on weapon

SERIAL KILLER WEAPONS & LABELS.
For Mr. Grave's collection of serial killer weapons, use any assortment of tools you own, such as a small saw, screwdriver, worker's gloves, etc. Make a label for each weapon assigning it to a real-life serial killer. For example:

- Noose: Cincinnati Strangler   • Axe: Lizzie Bordon
- Kitchen Knife: Jeffrey Dahmer   • Knife Sharpener: Ed Gein
- Saw: Jeffrey Dahmer   • Worker's Gloves: Henry Lee Lucas
- Winchester Knife: The Phantom Killer   • Dagger: Charles Manson
- Screwdriver: Ted Bundy

Place the labeled weapons on a shelf or desk in the spare room and leave a large **blank space** where an axe was once placed. *(When setting these up, remember to take special care that weapons are completely out of harms way so that no one will accidentally bump into them!)*

ROOM CARDS.
In the first half of the game, players will each search a single room or area of the house for clues. In order to determine who searches which room, photocopy the Room cards below and tape each to a 3 × 5" index card **cut in half**, labeling each with a different room. Put the cards in a black gift bag to keep hidden in the parlor.

PLACE CARDS.
Other items to make out of index cards are Place cards for the dinner table. Place cards can also be photocopied below and taped onto plain index cards. The last Place card has been left blank to be labeled either Roxy or Ox. Arrange the cards on the dinner table to sit woman-man-woman, sitting your guests next to anyone they have not met before whenever possible—keeping in mind that in this game, *no one* has met before!

STRAWS AND NOTEBOOKS. For the second part of the game, players will search the entire house with a partner. To assign partners, cut 4 long straws into different lengths so that each has a match.

Next, purchase 8 small notebooks and pens for players to write down any clues throughout the game. Place them in the parlor for players to take when they arrive.

WHAT REALLY HAPPENED. Finally, photocopy *What Really Happened* to reveal the killer's identity, murder weapon and murder location at the end of the party. *(Don't read it if you don't want to know the ending!)* Seal it in a white envelope labeled *What Really Happened* and hide in a desk drawer in the parlor.

PLAYING THE GAME

To play the game, read through Roxy/Ox's Game Sheet for a step-by-step guide on when characters should give clues, discover weapons, search the house, have dinner and solve the crime. You'll see that as the host, you are the key character for moving the game along. You'll be the one to discover Mr. Grave's body, accuse everyone of being responsible for his death and lead the group through a series of scenarios until the killer is revealed.

Tips:

- To get players more comfortable in their character roles, stay in your character of Roxy or Ox for the entire game. Act truly surprised that Mr. Grave was murdered and turn on the guests with complete distrust. Make comments and judgments on each player as they try to prove their innocence and encourage everyone to ask you questions throughout the evening.
- You may wish to use rooms in the house that don't have clues in them to throw players off track. Use the basement, attic or even the garage to plant subtle clues that have nothing to do with the murder. You may find that players come up with new theories as to who the killer is and how they committed the crime!
- Play big band music throughout the house to add to the overall atmosphere of the 1940s.

MAKE THIS GAME YOUR OWN!

Make your game of Mr. Grave's Gathering *original by being as conservative or elaborate with Roxy or Ox's personality and dress as you like. You may decide that your character is very loud and outspoken or very quiet and mysterious. You can also alter the décor to reflect the way you see Mr. Grave's taste, or make a large, more elaborate display of the collection of serial killer weapons.*

LIKE THIS GAME?

Check out The Nightly Haunt *in Chapter 5 for a deadly murder mystery with no script. The end result: there could be multiple killers among the group ... and there's no telling just who will see the light of day again!*

Invitation

_____, 1947

Dear Friend:

 I am pleased to invite you to an evening for the finest citizens of Washington, D.C. It is to be a night for those who find themselves in a most unfortunate circumstance, and wrongfully disgraced in the public eye.

 I think you will find it to be in your greatest interest to attend this friendly dinner on _____. For your own privacy, you have also been assigned an alias for the evening, being only known as _____.

 Please arrive promptly at _____.

Until then,

A Friend

Murder Mystery Dinner Party

Dear Party Guest:

 Greetings, Murder Mystery player! Enclosed you will find the Character Biography of the role you will be playing in *Mr. Grave's Gathering*. In this game, you will meet a variety of characters that come together for a most unusual evening in the year 1947. Throughout the night, you will all share dark secrets, search a strange mansion for clues and ultimately discover a **killer** among you.

 As one of the main characters, you will find it more fun to play the game if you are familiar with all the information in your Character Biography. This way, you can answer questions in the game quickly and absorb the information of others more easily.

 The information in your Character Biography is **all** that is known of your character's background. Nothing new will be added to your role during the game. Therefore, you are free to make up any additional background information or personality traits you wish to make your character unique.

 At the party, you will be given a sheet listing which information and clues to reveal at specific times throughout the game. However, all the information will be the same as in your Character Biography.

 Thanks for playing and see you soon!

Character Biography: Mr. Fox

You're 33 and worked as a top security guard at Safe Guard Bank for the past 5 years. You know everyone who works there, and just about everyone who has an account there. One such customer is a wealthy older man named Mr. Grave, who was always polite to you and other employees.

Six months ago, the bank was broken into on a Thursday (one of your regular days off) and the crooks got away with $50,000. Soon after, you got an anonymous letter asking you to switch your days off to Mondays, along with a check for $5,000. You were promised an additional $25,000 if you complied.

You switched your days off, telling the owners that Mondays would be better since the bank doesn't have much business then. Three months later, the bank was broken into on a Monday. The robbers got away with $75,000, but you never got a dime.

After the second robbery, you were questioned by the police as to your exact whereabouts at the time of both robberies. You had a solid alibi on both accounts: you were at the park with your son. However, the owners of the bank put you on unpaid leave until the robbers were found, which has yet to happen.

Today, your former co-workers are looking at you with suspicion as rumors spread throughout the entire bank of your possible involvement in the crimes.

You may *make up* any additional information not listed here, such as:
- The types of people you worked for
- Suspicions that co-workers or your bosses held against you

Character Dress: Please wear a shirt with one button missing.

COPY @ 120%

Character Biography: Mr. Knight

You are 28 and a reporter who has made it big in Washington D.C. You started out very poor, mostly interviewing small business owners and private collectors in the city. Then 2 years ago while you were out late, you overheard a man on a pay phone say he was going to kill someone in a few hours. You didn't believe him but you followed him anyway, secretly hoping that he *would* kill someone because a murder would be a hot story.

The man stabbed someone in the back a few hours later. You called the cops, but only after taking pictures and writing up the whole story. Ever since then, you've followed the killer around on almost a nightly basis. You've never called the cops, but the 13 crime scenes you've been fortunate enough to stumble upon have made you the top reporter in Washington. You even pinned the name for the killer: the D.C. Dicer.

However, you've been questioned by the police 6 times as to how you are able to find out about the killings so quickly. They ask where you were at the time of the murders, how you happened to be in that area and if you have any ideas about the identity of the D.C. Dicer. You always claim that you're constantly on the lookout after hours, since this is when you know you'll find the hot stories for the papers, and it's not your fault that the other reporters are too clueless to do it this way.

But lately, even the people you work with are starting to get nervous, as well as your friends, neighbors, and the general public of Washington.

A few months ago, you met a man named Mr. Grave when interviewing him for a story on his unusual collection of serial killer weapons. You were sent there by your boss, even though you tried to pass off the story to a "smaller" reporter. Mr. Grave commented in a sly tone how you were able to stumble upon local murders so quickly, and that he knew you had been interrogated by the cops about it more than once. You shrugged it off, and haven't seen Mr. Grave since.

You may *make up* any additional information not listed here, such as:
• The description of the D.C. Dicer
• The way the D.C. Dicer kills his victims

Character Biography:
Mr. Wolfe

You are 28 years old and worked as a driver during World War II. When the war ended and you came back to Washington, you were out of work and flat broke for 6 months. You almost got evicted from your apartment, then found out there was a lot of money to be made as a spy for the government. You uncovered people who had escaped the draft, who had helped *others* escape the draft and ratted out those who were secretly communists. You've also accepted bribes from people to keep their secrets quiet. You have big money now, and don't mind turning in even the most honest people to make some easy cash.

About a year ago, some friends of a man you turned in found you on the street and beat you severely. They had a knife, and they almost killed you when a police car drove by and scared them away. This event hasn't kept you from turning people in, but it has made you ready to kill anyone who tries to mess with you.

Shortly after the incident, you spied on a man named Mr. Grave. People in the black market wanted to know where and how he was getting his famous serial killer weapons. You found out that Mr. Grave knew some people in the forensic department of the FBI, and a lot of stuff made it to him without ever being missed. You can't be sure, but you think that Mr. Grave caught you spying on him, though you never met him face-to-face.

You may *make up* any additional information not listed here, such as:
- Specific people you turned in to the government
- How you were almost killed
- How you spied on Mr. Grave

Character Biography: Ms. Herring

You're 23 and have worked as a lowly paid chef for 6 years. You've always had a dream of becoming a Head Chef, and eventually owning your own restaurant. Six months ago, a job opening for a Head Chef came up at Sty Fry Restaurant. You were interviewed but did not get the job. Instead, it went to some cheap little brat right out of culinary school.

You brooded over it for months, plotting revenge on the owners and running low on cash. You thought about burning the restaurant down, and then decided to kill the owners instead so you could have the restaurant for yourself. Two months ago, you snuck into their home and replaced some frozen meat with a few pounds you had heavily poisoned. The couple died a few days later, and Sty Fry sold for half its worth. You borrowed money from a loan shark and bought it that very day. The first thing you did was fire the Head Chef.

But the story got into the papers of how you acquired the restaurant so quickly, and that you had been turned down for the Head Chef position not long before. You're not positive, but you're pretty sure that the ex–Head Chef leaked the story to the press. Ever since then, the customer flow has dropped considerably and your own staff is afraid of you.

A few weeks ago, you met a strange man who came into Sty Fry for dinner. He asked for you specifically and commented on the newspaper article, which you found very rude. He slyly said how he was looking forward to his meal. You never saw him again.

You may *make up* any additional information not listed here, such as:
• The restaurant where you worked before buying Sty Fry
• Description of previous Sty Fry owners
• Description of the previous Head Chef

Character Biography: Mr. Hawke

You are 18 and an arms dealer. You were a free-loading teenager until the beginning of World War II, at which time you started selling weapons to people all over Washington. You mostly dealt to those running off to Canada or the woods to escape the draft, but you've also done business with drug dealers, thugs, and just about anyone else to make a buck.

About 3 weeks ago, you read an article in the paper about a strange old man named Mr. Grave who had an unusual collection of weapons used by serial killers. You decided to sneak into his house one night to see if there was anything you could swipe and sell for a good price. However, before you could find the weapons Mr. Grave woke up and caught you. He didn't call the police, but demanded you tell him what you came there for. You lied and said you were homeless and just looking for some cash. Mr. Grave let you go, but you knew he didn't believe a word of it.

Ever since, you've seen someone out of the corner of your eye following you at least 3 times. You've tried to catch them, but they always disappear too quickly. You're pretty sure that Mr. Grave hired them to tail you and eventually turn you in to the cops.

When you received the invitation to the party, you arrived an hour early and killed Mr. Grave, knowing full well he was planning on blackmailing you now that he knows your line of work.

You may *make up* any additional information not listed here, such as:
- Things you did as a free-loading teenager
- Types of weapons you deal

Character Dress: Please wear blue jeans with a tear in them.

COPY @ 120%

Character Biography: Ms. Dove

You are 16 years old. You ran away from home when you were 14 and have been living in Washington, D.C., ever since. You made friends with your landlord, Tony, who was kind enough to lend you rent money for the last 3 months while you looked for work. The last time you saw Tony was 2 months ago, and he was becoming quite insistent that you pay him back. It ended in a heated argument that many people in the apartment building overheard.

The next day, you went to Tony's to apologize and give him the last of your money, covering one month's rent. As soon as you got there, he confessed that he needed the money to pay back a gambling debt. In desperation, he had borrowed over $10,000 from a loan shark to try and win enough money to get both of you on your feet. Suddenly, two men who had been hiding in another room busted in and shot Tony to death, telling him that he should have paid his debt on time. The men hadn't seen you, but you *had* been seen entering the apartment by quite a few neighbors, while the killers had been seen by no one. Rather than running to the police, you fled.

About 3 weeks ago, you met a man named Mr. Grave on the street. He could see that you had no where to live, so he treated you to lunch and asked about your situation. Feeling vulnerable, you told him everything. He had to leave rather abruptly afterwards, and you regretted what you had said.

You may *make up* any additional information not listed here, such as:
- Why you ran away from home at 14
- Where you were looking for work before your landlord was killed
- Description of your landlord

Character Biography: Miss Fog

You are 13 years old and used to live next door to a man named Mr. Grave. For years you never actually met him, but saw him from your yard every once in a while.

Six months ago, you found your parents murdered and decapitated in their bed. You panicked and — not knowing their heads were severed — screamed and tried to shake them awake. The next thing you remember, the cops arrived, you were covered in blood and had completely forgotten where you were and what you were doing before finding your parents. To make matters worse, the police found a bloody axe in your room with no fingerprints on it.

Later that day while the cops scouted the place, you met Mr. Grave face-to-face for the first time. He snuck in the back door and asked about the murders. You don't remember much of the conversation, but you remember that he seemed to suggest that *you* had killed your parents and simply blocked out the memory of it all afterwards.

A week later, you were placed in a foster home rather than being allowed to stay with relatives. You were also put on weekly surveillance by the city's social workers, and continue to be on surveillance to this day.

You may *make up* any additional information not listed here, such as:
- Description of your parents
- Description of your home
- Description of your foster parents

Character Dress: Please wear a coat with feathers on it and shorts/a skirt with dirt on one knee.

Game Sheet: Mr. Fox

(Your future pseudonym in the movie *Clue*: The Cop)

The Big Envelope:

- **Ask Mr. Knight** after his information is read: How many murders?
- **Answer in your defense when questioned by Mr. Hawke:** $125,000 total. But I had nothing to do with either of those robberies. I don't know who did it, but I'll find out to get my job back. The bank owners have me on unpaid leave until they're caught.
- *Ask any additional questions or make comments if you wish.*

Searching a Room:

- *Look for clues as to where the murder could have taken place, by whom and with what weapon.*

Dinner:

- **Ask Mr. Wolfe:** So what's it like ratting people out to the government?
- **When asked by Mr. Wolfe:** The first robbery happened 6 months ago, when I had Thursdays off work. They robbed the bank on a Thursday. After that, I changed my days off to Mondays, the slowest day at the bank. Three months later, the bank was robbed on a Monday. I have a solid alibi for both days: I was at the park with my son.

When asked how you knew Mr. Grave:

- I knew Mr. Grave because he had an account at Safe Guard Bank. I've made chit chat with him on dozens of accounts. He always seemed nice enough, in a reserved sort of way. Mr. Grave seemed to get along fine with everyone who worked at the bank. I also knew of him from the article in the paper about his odd collection.
- **At the time of the murder**, I was driving to the party.

Comment while Searching the House with a Partner:

- There's no way I'm the killer, though the people at that stupid bank would probably say so. I know everyone that works there and everyone who has an account there, and look what happens. Besides, that **Ms. Dove** looks like a drug addict if I ever saw one. People like that do desperate things.
- *After the search, discuss with the group any clues you found around the house and any information you got from your partner.*

Final Question:

- **Ask Ms. Dove:** You said you didn't kill your landlord, that he was killed over a gambling debt. If he was really in debt, how could he possibly have lent you any money?
- **When questioned by Ms. Dove:** After the first robbery, I was given $5,000 in an anonymous letter to switch my days off to Monday. I was promised an additional $25,000 after a second robbery would be done. But afterwards, the robbers never paid. Although they are probably miles away by now, I know it was probably **Mr. Grave** who spread rumors around the bank that I was involved in the crimes. He was a regular customer there, and it would give him a reason to blackmail me. But like I said from the beginning, I wasn't responsible for the robberies, now was I?

Game Sheet: Mr. Knight

(Your future pseudonym in the movie *Clue*: Wadsworth)

The Big Envelope:

- **Ask Ms. Dove** after her information is read: How much money had he lent you?
- **Say in your defense when questioned by Mr. Fox:** 13. I'm able to fall upon stories of murders so often because I'm constantly out after dark, since this is when I'm sure to find hot stories. Any *good* reporter would know that.
- *Ask any additional questions or make comments if you wish.*

Searching a Room:

- *Look for clues as to where the murder could have taken place, by whom and with what weapon.*

Dinner:

- **Ask Ms. Herring:** Did you have your eye on that restaurant you bought before the murders?
- **When asked by Mr. Hawke:** I've been questioned 6 times by the police since all of the murders have been within a 10 mile radius of my home within the past 2 months. I've fallen short of an alibi on more than one account (since sometimes I was alone), but I've never been charged since fingerprints were found that did not match my own. *Comment on how Mr. Fox has a button missing from his shirt.*

When asked how you knew Mr. Grave:

- I met Mr. Grave a few months ago when interviewing him for a story on his serial killer weapons collection. My boss sent me, even though I tried to pass it off to a *smaller* reporter. Mr. Grave commented on how I was able to stumble upon local murders so quickly, and that he knew I had been interrogated by the cops about it more than once. I shrugged it off, and haven't seen him since.
- **At the time of the murder**, I was stopping at a gas station to get gas.

Comment while Searching the House with a Partner:

- There's no way I'm the killer. I'm just a reporter who knew he'd make it big one day. I've been poor most of my life, it's not like I haven't earned it. Besides, I saw **Ms. Herring** shudder when she saw the poison vile in one of the weapon boxes.
- *After the search, discuss with the group any clues you found around the house and any information you got from your partner.*

Final Question:

- **Ask Mr. Wolfe:** In all this time you've been ratting people out, you never had anyone come after you for revenge?
- **When questioned by Mr. Wolfe:** The first time I found a murder victim, I had actually followed the guy who did it because I overheard him say he'd kill someone. Rather than call the cops, I followed him to see if he'd do it so I could get the story. Ever since then, I've been watching the city at night for any more crimes — but mostly I've been watching the killer.

COPY @ 120%

Game Sheet: Mr. Wolfe

(Your future pseudonym in the movie *Clue*: The Motorist)

The Big Envelope:
- **Ask Mr. Hawke** after his information is read: You're an arms dealer?
- **Say in your defense when questioned by Ms. Herring:** People who ran from the draft or helped others run from the draft. Communists. Hey, there's nothing wrong with what I do. People like that are asking for it anyway.
- *Ask any additional questions or make comments if you wish.*

Searching a Room:
- *Look for clues as to where the murder could have taken place, by whom and with what weapon.*

Dinner:
- **Comment to Mr. Fox:** It's quite a coincidence you weren't working at the bank either time it was robbed.
- **When asked by Mr. Fox:** I don't turn *everyone* in. If people have enough money, I take a sum from them, and then they're scott-free and I'm out of their lives forever. Hey, now that the war's over, it's hard to find work.

When asked how you knew Mr. Grave:
- I spied on Mr. Grave about a year ago. People in the black market wanted to know where and how he was getting so many weapons from famous serial killers. Turns out that Mr. Grave knew some people in the forensic department of the FBI, and a lot of stuff made it to him without ever being missed. I can't be sure, but I think that Mr. Grave caught me spying on him, but I never met him face-to-face.
- **At the time of the murder**, I was driving with Ms. Dove to the party, who had been hitchhiking.

Comment while Searching the House with a Partner:
- I'm not the killer. I'm just out to make a buck, that's all. When I got back from the war, I was out of work for 6 months and about to be out on the street. Besides, I saw **Miss Fog** eyeing the weapons in the boxes several times before dinner.
- *After the search, discuss with the group any clues you found around the house and any information you got from your partner.*

Final Question:
- **Ask Mr. Knight**: It seems awfully odd that you just *happen* to stumble upon all these murders, even if you're not the killer. Did you know who the killer was all this time?
- **When asked by Mr. Knight:** About a year ago, I was almost killed by friends of someone I turned in for hiding draft dodgers. They hurt me pretty bad, but the police drove by just in time and the men fled. If anyone tried to do that again, I would kill them for sure.

Game Sheet: Ms. Herring

(Your future pseudonym in the movie *Clue*: The Cook)

The Big Envelope:
- **Ask Mr. Wolfe** after his information is read: What kind of crimes?
- **Say in your defense when questioned by Miss Fog:** Food poisoning. I had nothing to do with the death of the previous owners of Sty Fry. It was probably just bad meat they bought. Food poisoning happens all the time.
- *Ask any additional questions or make comments if you wish.*

Searching a Room:
- *No matter which room you're assigned, keep an eye out for any **drinks** in Mr. Grave's **bedroom** or **spare room**. If you find anything, **hide it** so that no one thinks Mr. Grave was poisoned, as your true past with the previous Sty Fry owners is sure to come out.*

Dinner:
- **Ask Mr. Hawke:** Do you really only sell weapons to people running from the war? *(Also, comment on the strange tear in his pants.)*
- **When asked by Mr. Knight:** I had been interviewed for the job of Head Chef at Sty Fry six months ago, but I didn't get it. Four months later, the "accident" happened, the place sold for half its worth, and I was able to get a loan through a loan shark that very day. I fired the Head Chef and the next thing I know, the story's in the papers.

When asked how you knew Mr. Grave:
- I met Mr. Grave when he came into Sty Fry one evening for dinner. He asked for me specifically, and commented on the newspaper article about me, which I found very rude. He slyly said how he was looking forward to his meal.
- **At the time of the murder,** I was checking on the staff at my restaurant to make sure all was in order.

Comment while Searching the House with a Partner:
- I'm not the killer. I'm just someone who's always wanted to be a Head Chef. And look where I am now: my own customers and staff are afraid of me because of all this scandal. Besides, it seems awfully suspicious that **Mr. Fox's** bank was robbed when there was so much money in the vaults those days.
- *After the search, discuss with the group any clues you found around the house and any information you got from your partner.*

Final Question:
- **Ask Miss Fog:** It seems awfully convenient that a person could completely block out the memory of murdering their parents. Have the police never questioned you again for your alibi at the time of their death?
- **When questioned by Mr. Hawke:** After the owners turned me down for the Head Chef job, I brooded over how to kill them without getting caught. I thought about burning the place down, but decided it would be much better if the restaurant remained in tact, so I broke into their kitchen, switched some meat with a few pounds I'd poisoned, and they were dead within days.

COPY @ 120%

Game Sheet: Mr. Hawke

(Your future pseudonym in the movie *Clue*: Mr. Boddy)

The Big Envelope:

- **Ask Mr. Fox** after his information is read: How much was stolen from the bank?
- **Say in your defense when questioned by Mr. Wolfe**: I mainly deal to people who ran from the war. People need protection. Who wouldn't need a gun to save themselves from being sent off to die for nothing? If it were me, I'd do the same thing.
- *Ask any additional questions or make comments if you wish.*

Searching a Room:

- *No matter which room you're assigned, sneak into the* **bathroom** *and find a box of feathers and buttons in the medicine cabinet. Get a feather that matches* **the color of Miss Fog's coat** *and plant it on* **Mr. Grave's suit**. *Get a button that matches* **the color of Mr. Fox's jacket** *and plant it among the serial killer weapons collection.*

Dinner:

- **Ask Mr. Knight:** What do the police think of your ability to find so many murders?
- **When asked by Ms. Herring:** I don't *only* sell to people running from the draft, but they're a big percentage of my revenue. I'll sell to anyone else who comes to me. Hey, it's not my business what they do. (*If asked,* lie *and say your pants got torn on a branch by the road when you were working on your car before you arrived.*)

When asked how you knew Mr. Grave:

- I met Mr. Grave when I snuck into his house one night to swipe some of his famous weapons. He woke up and caught me but didn't turn me in, probably because there was nothing in it for him. I told him I was a homeless bum. He didn't buy it, but he still let me go.
- **At the time of the murder:** Lie *and say you were trying to fix your engine.*

Comment while Searching the House with a Partner:

- *Try to convince your partner you're not the killer:* Hey, I'm just someone trying to make a buck off the war. Who wouldn't? Mr. Grave must have, in his own way. Besides, that **Mr. Knight** seems pretty sick. Who goes out looking for murders, anyway?
- *After the search, discuss with the group any clues you found and information you heard that make it look like* someone else *is the killer.*

Final Question:

- **Ask Ms. Herring:** It seems awfully suspicious the previous owners of your restaurant would have bad meat in their home, and that a Head Chef they turned down for a job would buy up the place so quickly afterwards. What's the real reason Mr. Grave believed he could blackmail you?
- **When asked by Miss Fog:** *Confess that you know Mr. Grave sent someone to spy on you, since you saw someone following you on a few occasions. It was probably Mr. Grave's assistant (the host), now that you know what they do.* Lie *and say you didn't kill Mr. Grave. Someone else beat you to it.*
- **When and if** *the other guests find out you're the killer, threaten to take each of their situations to the newspapers and the cops: making them* all *look like killers and thieves, as they are all under suspicion already...*

Game Sheet: Ms. Dove

(Your future pseudonym in the movie *Clue*: Yvette)

The Big Envelope:

- **Ask Miss Fog** after her information has been read: Did you see who killed your parents?
- **Say in your defense when questioned by Mr. Knight**: Three months rent. I didn't shoot my landlord. I had been in his apartment when 2 men came out from hiding and shot him over a gambling debt. I fled because the police never would have believed me.
- *Ask any additional questions or make comments if you wish.*

Searching a Room:

- *Look for clues as to where the murder could have taken place, by whom and with what weapon.*

Dinner:

- **Ask Miss Fog:** Why would the police insist on putting you under surveillance if you had nothing to do with the murder of your parents? *(Also, comment that her knee is scraped up.)*
- **When asked by Miss Fog:** My landlord and I had been in an argument the night before, which several neighbors overheard. I went to his apartment to pay him one month's rent when some men came out and shot him. Several neighbors had seen me enter the apartment, but no one had seen these men. I knew the police wouldn't believe my story.

When asked how you knew Mr. Grave:

- I met Mr. Grave on the street about 3 weeks ago. He could see that I had no where to live, so he treated me to lunch and asked about my situation. I was feeling completely vulnerable and just told him everything. He left pretty quickly afterwards, and I regretted what I had said.
- **At the time of the murder**, I was hitchhiking to get a ride to the party, and Mr. Wolfe picked me up.

Comment while Searching the House with a Partner:

- I'm not the killer. When I saw my landlord shot, I almost puked. I'm glad that the guys who killed him didn't see *me*, though. I think that **Mr. Grave's assistant** sure knows a lot about everyone here tonight.
- *After the search, discuss with the group any clues you found around the house and any information you got from your partner.*

Final Question:

- **Ask Mr. Fox:** It seems odd that Mr. Grave would have any reason to blackmail you if you really had nothing to do with those robberies. What would make him so sure that you'd even pay?
- **When questioned by Mr. Fox:** My landlord really did have a gambling problem. He admitted it just before he was killed, and told me he borrowed over $10,000 from a loan shark to try and get both of us out of debt for good, which is how he could let me slide on the rent.

COPY @ 120%

Game Sheet: Miss Fog
(Your future whereabouts in the movie *Clue*: The Telegram Girl)

The Big Envelope:
- **Ask Ms. Herring** after her information is read: How did they die?
- **Say in your defense when questioned by Ms. Dove:** I don't know ... I don't remember anything of that day, other than finding my parents dead in their bed. I can't be sure, but I don't think I was home at the time they were killed.
- *Ask any additional questions or make comments if you wish.*

Searching a Room:
- *No matter which room you're assigned,* **sneak around** *until you find the collection of serial killer weapons you've heard about. When you see it, you realize that it was* **Mr. Grave** *who killed your parents. Keep this to yourself, but* **steal** *something from the collection with the attempt to frame* **Mr. Hawke**—*who also deals in weapons and is therefore probably the killer.*

Dinner:
- **Ask Ms. Dove:** Why did you think the police wouldn't believe you weren't the one who killed your landlord?
- **When asked by Ms. Dove:** When I found my parents, I didn't understand they were dead, I thought they were just unconscious, so I tried shaking them awake. When the cops came, I was covered in blood and they found a bloody axe in my room. I've never seen that axe before. They put me in a foster home a week later when they found no fingerprints on it. *(If asked:)* My knee is scraped up due to school sports.

When asked how you knew Mr. Grave:
- Mr. Grave was my neighbor. My old house is to the right of this one. I'd seen Mr. Grave on several occasions growing up, but the first time I actually met him was the day my parents were killed, when he stopped by the house and snuck past the cops. He asked me about the murders and seemed to suggest that I had committed them, and simply blocked out the memory of it all.
- **At the time of the murder,** I was getting a ride to the party from my foster parents. I lied and told them it was a birthday party for a friend.

Comment while Searching the House with a Partner:
- I'm not the killer, so why am I constantly surrounded by death? First my parents are killed and decapitated, and now this. Anyway, that **Mr. Hawke** guy is freaky. Anyone who deals with guns is a killer for sure.
- *After the search, discuss with the group any clues you found around the house and any information you got from your partner.*

Final Question:
- **Ask Mr. Hawke:** If Mr. Grave caught you breaking into his house and he just let you go, I doubt that you never saw him again after that. Did you?
- **When asked by Ms. Herring:** No. But I know now who killed them. It was Mr. Grave. I saw the area among his collection of weapons where a big axe used to be placed. It was the same size axe that they found in my room when my parents were killed. I'm glad Mr. Grave is dead, and I wish I *had* done it!

Female Character: Roxy or Male Character: Ox

(Host of the party and character within it. No future character in *Clue*.)

1. GUESTS ARRIVE. When the guests arrive, introduce them by their character name and give them their Game Sheet. State that all the information they'll need for the game is on their Game Sheet, which includes when they should ask other players specific questions and when they should answer questions. Each person should also feel free to ask *you* any questions throughout the game. Players should read through their *entire* sheet before the game begins.

2. FINDING THE BODY. Once everyone has arrived, reveal that they are all being addressed by a pseudonym for their own privacy. (If anyone asks, you don't know about the gift boxes on the coffee table, but you *do* know that just a little while ago none of them were opened.) Question where Mr. Grave could be, growing suspicious since you saw him just an hour ago. Go to the closet to see if his coat is still in there and find his body stuffed inside. Announce that he has no visible wounds, but a trace of blood is coming from his head. It doesn't look like he was shot, but rather like he was hit by something.

3. THE FIRST CLUES. Inform everyone that Mr. Grave was alive only an hour ago, and that someone here tonight must have snuck in at some point and **killed him**. Anyone here could have done it, since his address was listed on their invitations and his body was obviously put away to keep hidden. *No one* leaves until they figure out what happened. However, you think you know *why* Mr. Grave was killed. Announce that each person was called here tonight because Mr. Grave found them most interesting for one reason or another.

Go to the big envelope with your name on it and announce that Mr. Grave instructed you to read its contents aloud at his request, which you will do now, as you suspect it will help solve the question of who killed him. Read the information about each person, allowing everyone time to ask questions and defend themselves. After revealing the clues of all 7 guests, tell the group information about Mr. Grave, and then yourself:

- **Mr. Grave was a wealthy, 50 year-old man who lived here in Washington D.C. He was known throughout the city for his unusual collection of weapons used by both convicted and unidentified serial killers, which has put him in the papers more than once.**
- *I've worked for Mr. Grave for 3 years as a special assistant, while also agreeing to arrange his "social gatherings." This has been the first of such gatherings in the entire time I've worked for him.*
- (If asked by anyone:) *I am a paid informant for Mr. Grave. And yes, I did gather all this information about each of you. Mr. Grave was very eccentric and seemed to be intrigued by crime and murder.* (If asked specifically, you do not believe Mr. Grave's intentions for bringing everyone here tonight were corrupt.)

Once everyone's info is out in the open, say that someone here must have killed Mr. Grave because he or she believed they were brought here tonight to be **blackmailed**.

4. THE WEAPONS. State that the gift boxes on the coffee table must have been opened around the time of the murder. Encourage the guests to open them and be genuinely surprised that they contain weapons, since only Mr. Grave had handled them. Allow the guests to ponder which weapons look used and which do not, and announce that one of them must have been used to kill Mr. Grave. Contemplate why Mr. Grave would have given them each a weapon. Then, go to the body of Mr. Grave and find a gun in his pocket.

5. THE ROOM SEARCH. Since no one will be leaving until the killer is discovered, insist that everyone have dinner, since you had to make it all, damn it, and they're going to eat it. Announce that you'll get everything ready in the dining area, in which time each person should search one room of the house to look for clues as to **where** Mr. Grave was killed, with **what** weapon and by **whom**. To determine who goes where, have each player choose a Room card from the black bag. (You won't need a card since you'll be getting the dinner table ready and setting out Place cards during this time.) Everyone should meet for dinner in 20 minutes.

6. DINNER. During dinner, encourage the guests to talk about anything suspicious they came across throughout the house, and if it could point to who killed Mr. Grave, in what room and with what weapon. Make sure everyone asks each other questions about their pasts. With each answer, make judgments on what people say and encourage others to do the same.

Reveal if asked by anyone **if** the blackmailing letter has been found:

Okay, I knew that Mr. Grave had blackmailed people to get most of his money. And there was a chance that you were all called here to get blackmailed. I've been spying on everyone here for the past year, but it was Mr. Grave who found out about you in the first place. Mr. Grave's obsession with weapons and serial killers was probably why he had those boxes of weapons for you in the parlor. He wanted to see you panic and try to attack him or even each other, so he would have a body count of his own. (This is the only information you know of Mr. Grave)

Reveal if asked by anyone if the blackmailing letter has **not** been found:

I've been spying on everyone here for the past year, but it was Mr. Grave who found out about you all in the first place. I didn't think he was planning on blackmailing anyone, but then again, it wasn't my business to ask. I just know he liked serial killer stuff, and spent tons of money on it. I simply thought Mr. Grave liked people involved in crime and murder. He was, after all, quite eccentric. (Reveal the information above when the blackmailing letter is found.)

7. ACQUAINTANCES WITH MR. GRAVE. After dinner, ask everyone just how they knew Mr. Grave and where they were at the time of his murder.

How you knew Mr. Grave:

I met Mr. Grave 3 years ago when my private investigation business was falling under. He gave me the proposition of being a paid informant strictly for him, and for a very good salary. Times were tough, and since it didn't require doing anything unethical, I took the job.

At the time of the murder, I was off chasing the dogs that had gotten loose from their chains out front. I left and entered the house again through the front door, but the dogs were never found.

8. THE HOUSE SEARCH. With the supposed alibis revealed, announce that the killer has still not been unmasked, but everyone here is most certainly a criminal. For further clues, everyone should complete the search of the house, this time searching the *entire* house. You'll go on this search, as well, especially since the guests have said what is supposedly in each room. However, everyone will split into pairs so that no one can attempt to hide or change any existing evidence. Take out the straws and have everyone draw to form teams of two. Tell everyone to share any thoughts with their search partner as to who they think the killer may be and why. However, if anyone should find that their partner is the one they will be making a comment about, they should find *someone else* to tell it to in passing. Everyone should meet in the parlor in 30 minutes.

While searching the house with your partner, comment on the following:

I would never have killed Mr. Grave, he was always nice to me. I had to see all kinds of horrible things as a private investigator before I met him, so thank goodness he found me and bailed me out. I've also been thinking that Mr. Wolfe is a pretty big guy, and looks like someone who could drag a body around pretty easily.

9. FINAL CLUES. Once everyone gathers back in the parlor, announce that you just heard on the radio that the serial killer Mr. Knight has been writing stories about has been caught and denied ever having an accomplice, putting Mr. Knight in the all-clear of being the murderer.

Encourage everyone to talk about any additional clues they found around the house and if it helps point to who committed the murder, where and with what. Also, ask each player to reveal any information they got from their partner during the search.

Finally, each player will ask and answer a final question.

10. POINTING FINGERS. With all the clues out in the open, ask everyone to make their guess as to who the killer is, where the murder was done, and with what weapon.

11. WHODUNIT. Read "What Really Happened."

12. SECRET IDENTITIES. Tell players to reveal which character they actually are from the movie *Clue*.

COPY @ 120%

Clues for the Big Envelope

Mr. Knight, you are 28 years old and — it's safe to say — the most questionable reporter in Washington, D.C. You were once a common reporter for the city, covering small, local events that never made it to the front page. Yet lately your stories have come to be quite well known, since for the past 2 years you've been the only one to stumble upon a series of gruesome murders from the so-called D.C. Dicer.

Ms. Dove, you are 16 years old and ran away from home when you were only 14. You were doing alright for yourself in your quiet apartment in Washington until recently, when your landlord was shot down in his apartment, just a few doors down from your own. This landlord had also lent you quiet a lot of money not long before his death. When he was killed you fled immediately rather than going to the police.

Mr. Hawke, you are 18 years old and were a bit of a free-loafing teenager until the beginning of the Second World War. Ever since that time, you have been quite well known throughout Washington — for those who know where to find you — with a steady business of acquiring firearms and distributing them to those currently in need. Your business practices also have you currently wanted by the police.

Mr. Wolfe, you are 28 years old and previously had a very honorable assignment as a driver in the Second World War. However, ever since the war ended you've chosen work that is slightly less admirable, spying on your fellow civilians and turning them in to the government for small crimes.

Mr. Fox, you are 33 years old and for the past 5 years have worked as a top security guard at Safe Guard Bank, one of the most widely used and trusted banks in Washington. Yet, you have recently been relieved of your duties due to the fact that the bank was robbed not once, but twice over the past 6 months, and both times when you were off duty.

Ms. Herring, you are 23 years old and a trained chef. Having tried and failed to land a steady job as Head Chef in several restaurants in Washington, your funds were starting to run quite low. Yet recently you acquired ownership of a high-end restaurant in the city after the owners suddenly died.

Miss Fog, you are 13 years old and were living a normal and happy childhood until you witnessed a most terribly tragedy. Six months ago you found your parents brutally murdered in their bedroom. After the incident, the authorities decided that rather than allow you to stay with relatives, to place you in foster care under surveillance, where you remain to this day.

Blackmail Letter

Mr. Grave —

You will find this month's payment enclosed. I hope you are satisfied, as you have completely drained my finances and subsequently ended my marriage. I am both pleased and dispirited to tell you that this will be the last payment you ever receive from me, as I am ending my life rather than go on with the knowledge of the things I have done.

May one of the many desperate souls you have extorted over the years one day take their revenge on you, as I cannot bring myself to do it.

See you in hell,

Arthur Appleton

Room Cards

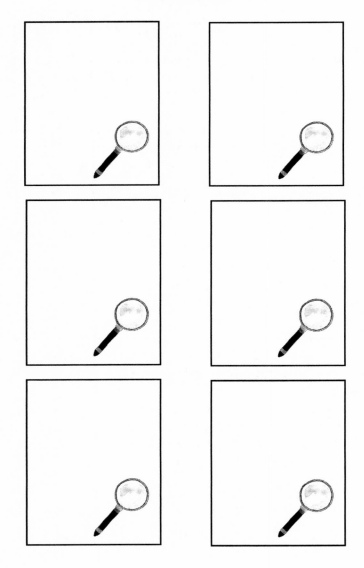

Place Cards

Miss Fog	Mr. Fox
Mr. Wolfe	Ms. Dove
Mr. Knight	Mr. Hawke
Ms. Herring	

WHAT REALLY HAPPENED

The killer of Mr. Grave was Mr. Hawke. Mr. Hawke recognized the address on the invitation as the home of Mr. Grave, where he had been just 3 weeks before. When Mr. Hawke received his invitation, he knew he was about to be blackmailed and that whoever had been following him had seen him selling weapons. He also knew he'd be looking at some serious jail time if he didn't either comply with Mr. Grave or kill him.

Mr. Hawke arrived an hour before the party was due to begin. He saw there was a servant in the house, so he untied the dogs out front so the servant would have to go get them. As the dogs ran past him they made a tear in his jeans.

While the servant was out chasing the dogs, Mr. Hawke snuck in the back door and walked through the parlor. Carrying no weapon so that an arms dealer wouldn't be suspected of the murder, he relied on using one of Mr. Grave's. However, he could hear Mr. Grave moving around upstairs, in between himself and the collection. He then saw the boxes on the coffee table and, knowing Mr. Grave's obsession, knew what would be inside. He opened them until he found something he wanted to use, putting each weapon on the table except the wrench, candlestick and switchblade. He then took the pipe, snuck up the stairs and killed Mr. Grave in the hall, catching him by surprise.

Mr. Hawke then dragged the body down the stairs with the intention of hiding it in the basement. But before he could reach it he heard the servant coming back. Mr. Hawke then stuffed Mr. Grave into the parlor closet and put the weapons back in their boxes, accidentally dripping blood on the poison vial and pipe and leaving a fingerprint on the dagger. He then snuck out the back door.

When everyone split up to search individual rooms, Mr. Hawke took a feather from Miss Fog's coat and a button from Mr. Fox's jacket and planted them around the house as false clues.

COPY @ 120%

8

THE ADDAMS CLAN PARTY

Dance Party and Display Game
based on *The Addams Family (1991)*,
8–14 players

    The Addams Family reinvents our favorite morbid family from the 1960s television show. Gomez, Morticia, Fester, Wednesday, Pugsly and Lurch may live in the most common of neighborhoods, but they're living in their own world of dungeons, graveyards and torture devices—all the things that make family time so special.

Perhaps the most intriguing thing about the Addams' is that they may seem to be the odd balls at first, but by the end of the film we realize the dark truth: that everyone else is crazy and *they* are the ones who know how to live!

THE GAME

At this party, players assume the roles of strange Addams' relatives who have come together for an entire clan party. Festivities include dance games in a torture chamber, detecting the owners of weird or deadly party favors, digging up long-lost relatives in the graveyard and taking part in a costume contest. You will need:

- 50–60 Gold Coins in a Small Bowl • 6–8 Completely Demented Prizes
- 5 pieces of Black Cardstock • 2 Small Tables • 2 Gray Tablecloths
- 2 Vases of Flower Stems

Dance Game: • 5 Scrap Pieces of Paper, each listing 1 of the following: Rack, Breaking Wheel, Electric Chair, Guillotine, Stocks
- Blank CD • Black Gift Bag

Cauldron Count: • Large Cauldron (8–9") • "Unusual Item"

Wake the Dead: • 15–20 Bones, Skulls & Body Parts • 2–3 Shovels
- Tombstone **for each Player** • Garbage Bag **for each Tombstone**
- Small Cloth Bag

Costume Contest: • Index Card **for each player** • Red Gift Bag

Torture Décor: • 2 Small Pieces of Rope • Fireplace Pokers
- Charcoal • White Cloth • Basket with Dismembered Head or Skull
- Bowl of Tomatoes and other Vegetables

Additional Supplies: • CD Burner • Scissors • Double-Sided Tape

PREPARING THE PARTY

To prepare for your Addams Clan Party, you'll need to put together the following:
- Invitations • Dance CD • Unusual Item • Party Décor • Dinner
- Costume • Host Sheet

INVITATIONS. Photocopy an invitation below for each guest, then tape each onto a 3¼ × 5" piece of black cardstock. Mail these out to your guests so they are informed of what to bring and warned of the grisly deeds to come.

DANCE CD. Make a party CD with the right tunes for your dance games, using any number of songs to make the games as long or short as you wish. Include songs from the film and other hits to match the timeframe, such as:
- Addam's Groove, MC Hammer • Move This, Technotronic
- Walk the Dinosaur, Was (Not Was) • Too Ligit to Quit, MC Hammer
- Just Got Paid, Johnny Kemp • Rock Steady, The Whispers
- Pump Up the Jam, Technotronic • Get Up Offa That Thing, James Brown
- Born to Be Alive, Patrick Hernandez

UNUSUAL ITEM. The Cauldron Count game involves players each contributing an unusual item they either made or bought, so don't forget to contribute one yourself. See the description of the game below for ideas on coming up with something twisted. You may want to use something that reflects the type of personality of your Addams character. Label your item with a tag that gives its brief description, such as where you got it or what you use it for.

PARTY DÉCOR. Décor for the party will help turn your house into a true Addams home and includes setting up a torture chamber in the Dance Room and an outdoor graveyard in the yard. Any other areas of the house you choose to deck out are up to your own demented imagination.

The Dance Room: Use the living room or other large room in the house for the Dance Room. Photocopy the Death & Torture images below and paste each onto an 8½ × 11" piece of black cardstock. Tape the images to different corners of the room and along a center wall. Hang or place a few props next to each image to better create the torture chamber atmosphere:
- *The Rack:* Small pieces of rope with loops at the end
- *The Breaking Wheel:* Fireplace pokers and pieces of charcoal
- *The Electric Chair:* A white cloth mask with 2 eyeholes cut out
- *The Guillotine:* A large basket containing a dismembered head or skull
- *The Stocks:* A small bowl of tomatoes and other vegetables

Next, set up 2 small tables in the Dance Room topped with gray tablecloths and vases of flower stems. On one table place the large cauldron for unusual items and on the other place the prizes, bowl of coins, black bag of torture items, red bag and index cards for the costume contest.

The Graveyard: To set up the graveyard for Wake the Dead, purchase or make a small Styrofoam tombstone for each player at the party — including yourself! Use black paint to write assorted names of late Addams' on each stone. Set the tombstones in the ground with thin metal rods and dig a shallow hole before each one.

Next, divide the skeleton bones into separate garbage bags so that there are a few in each bag but so that one bag has the most. Place the bags in a pile in the center of the graveyard, and put the small, cloth bag with coins inside one of them. Mix up the bags so that you don't remember which has how many bones in it. Then, empty each bag into the graves, trying not to look at what goes in so that you'll be just as surprised at what you dig up in the game as everyone else!

DINNER. This party includes dancing like crazy and digging up graves, and that can build up quite a monstrous appetite. Whether you decide to have a sit down dinner or an array of snacks, make sure you have some tasty treats at hand so players won't end up passing out in any open graves.

COSTUME. Since this party involves dressing as a strange Addams family member, prepare a costume that reflects any type of character you would like to be. You may want to dress in a ravishing and formal gothic style or go for more of a raggedy and murderous look. Whichever you choose, make yourself stand out as only a true Addams family member would.

HOST SHEET. Finally, photocopy the Host Sheet below to serve as a step-by-step guide for the night's events.

AT THE PARTY

As the guests arrive, ask them to leave their shovel outside and place their Unusual Item in the cauldron. Players should not let anyone see their item, and not look at the items that are already in the cauldron.

DANCE GAMES. Once everyone has arrived, start the party off with the Dance Games. These are played by letting everyone dance in any style they choose—completely normal or in a totally bizarre Addams style—to the songs on the dance CD. At the end of each song, all players (including you, the host) go to one of the 5 killing and torture areas of the room. One player then chooses a paper from the black bag and reads it aloud. Whoever is standing at the listed device wins a gold coin. At the end of the dance game, the one(s) with the most coins wins a prize and all coins are returned to the bowl.

FOOD AND VOTES. After dancing in the torture chamber, let everyone relax with some food and drinks. Players should also put in their ballad for best costume into the red bag at this time.

CAULDRON COUNT. Once players are good and stuffed, begin the Cauldron Count game. This is played by one person going to the cauldron and taking out an item without looking at the others. The player reads the item's label aloud, then tries to guess who brought it. If they guess correctly, they win a gold coin. If they don't, the item is left out on the table. The next player then chooses an item from the cauldron. If they do not correctly identify who brought it, they may then guess for one of the items already on the table. Players may only guess up to 2 items each turn: a new item from the cauldron and one on the table. If players guess correctly with the first item, they *cannot* guess for another. Once an item has been identified, it is put aside. The game is played until every item has been correctly assigned to its owner. At the end of the game, the one with the most coins wins a prize.

WAKE THE DEAD. After the Cauldron Count, invite everyone out in the graveyard for Wake the Dead. The game is played by each player choosing a tombstone, then digging up the grave to unearth the bones. Whoever finds the most bones and skulls wins a prize, as does the one who finds the small bag of gold coins.

COSTUME CONTEST. After returning from digging up graves, players return indoors for dessert and to count ballads for the Costume Contest. The winner is given the final prize.

MAKE THIS GAME YOUR OWN!

Alter future Addams Clan Parties *with new music, different kinds of prizes and specific themes for guests to work with in making their Unusual Items. You can also include an "Unusual Item Swap" so that players have the option of swapping their items with other players for a very strange parting gift!*

Invitation

You're invited to

The Addams Clan Party

This is a gathering for all **extended** members of the Addams Family:
all Siamese twins, unidentified sexes, gypsies and other
odd-balls that are proud to call themselves Addams!

Come to our humble gathering to enjoy food, dancing to tunes
of the 90s and our favorite family past-time: Wake the Dead!
Also, suit up in your most elaborate outfit for our Costume Contest!

Please Bring the Following:
• One drawing, bone or body part, weapon (fake only, please!) or other **unusual
item** for the Cauldron Count game. Attach a tag to your item briefly stating its
background story or purpose. *Please keep your item hidden in a bag when you arrive!*
• A shovel for Wake the Dead.

You're invited to

The Addams Clan Party

This is a gathering for all **extended** members of the Addams Family:
all Siamese twins, unidentified sexes, gypsies and other
odd-balls that are proud to call themselves Addams!

Come to our humble gathering to enjoy food, dancing to tunes
of the 90s and our favorite family past-time: Wake the Dead!
Also, suit up in your most elaborate outfit for our Costume Contest!

Please Bring the Following:
• One drawing, bone or body part, weapon (fake only, please!) or other **unusual
item** for the Cauldron Count game. Attach a tag to your item briefly stating its
background story or purpose. *Please keep your item hidden in a bag when you arrive!*
• A shovel for Wake the Dead.

Death & Torture

The Rack

The Breaking Wheel

The Stocks

The Guillotine

The Electric Chair

Host Sheet

AS GUESTS ARRIVE. Ask guests to leave their shovels outside and put their Unusual Items in the cauldron *without peeking* at what else is in there. Unusual items should not be seen by any other players!

DANCE GAMES. For each song in the dance games, everyone dances in whatever style they want — completely normal or in a totally bizarre Addams style. At the end of each song, players (including you, the host), go to 1 of the 5 Death & Torture devices in the room. One player chooses a paper from the black bag and reads it aloud. Anyone standing at the listed device wins a coin. The game continues for however many songs you choose. Once the games are over, the one(s) with the most coins wins a prize and players return their coins to the bowl.

DINNER. Everyone has dinner and puts their ballad for best costume in the red bag.

CAULDRON COUNT. One player goes to the cauldron and takes an item without peeking at the others. The player reads its label aloud and tries to guess who brought it. If they guess correctly, they win a gold coin. If they don't, the item is left on the table. The next player then chooses a new item from the cauldron. If they do not correctly identify who brought it, then may then guess for one of the items on the table. Players may only guess up to 2 items each turn: a new item from the cauldron and one on the table. If a player guesses correctly with the first item, they cannot guess for another. Once an item has been identified, it is put aside. The game is played until each item has been correctly identified. At the end of the game, the one with the most coins wins a prize.

WAKE THE DEAD. After the Cauldron Count, everyone goes out into the graveyard for Wake the Dead. Each player chooses a tombstone and digs up the grave to unearth bones. Whoever finds the most skulls and bones wins a prize, as does the one who finds the small bag of gold coins.

COSTUME CONTEST. Players return indoors for dessert and ballads are counted for the best costume. The winner is given the final prize.

9
WITCHES AND WARLOCKS

Spell Casting Board Game
based on *Hocus Pocus (1993)*,
2–4 players

Hocus Pocus paints a pretty different picture than what most of us envision of 17th century witches and witchcraft. Winifred, Mary and Sarah Sanderson aren't the innocent children of nature who heal the sick and perform white magic. These gals worship the Devil, eat children alive and conjure spells to live forever ... which is much more interesting than what's written in the history books!

In the film we hear a few excerpts from Winifred's spell book made out of human skin, but what other kinds of spells are in there? And what other horrid deeds would your typical witch or warlock be capable of once entrusted with its deadly components?

THE GAME

In this board and spell casting game, players take on the roles of a particular kind of witch or warlock to cast a spell of their own. They may be necromancers, deceptive, vain or hungry witches, each specializing in particular spell items to carry out their evil deeds. Players get their own spell book of dark magic to use for personal gain, causing mischief to the world and possibly to other players. You will need:

- 20 Gold Coins • 4 Colored Gem Stones • Sheet of White Poster Board
- Colored Pencils or Markers • Thin, Black Marker • Small Cauldron
- Regular Die
Spell Items: • 3 Stones • 2 Twigs • 2 Vials of Fake Blood • 2 Small Bones
- Small Black Skull • Small White Skull • Bag of Witch Hazel
- Bag of Garlic • Bag of Wormwood • Poison Vial • Brown Candle
- Black Candle • White Candle • Red Candle • Bat • Bag of Graveyard Dirt
- Rat
Additional Supplies: • Stapler

PREPARING THE GAME

To make *Witches and Warlocks,* you'll need to assemble the following:
- Game Board • Spell Book **for each Player**

GAME BOARD. To make the board for the game, cut an 11 x 11" square out of white poster board. Following the model below, draw a small circle in the center of the board with a larger circle around it. Mark out 24 spaces around the outer circle for the following:
- 13 Spider web spaces • 6 Tombstone spaces • 2 Cats Eye spaces
- 2 Burning Rain of Death spaces • 1 Begin space
In the smaller circle write "Witches and Warlocks" and draw images of a skull, bone, rat and candle. Outline the image with a thin black marker and color individual spaces with colored pencils or markers. For extra support, apply the board to a sheet of plywood so that it doesn't warp and it can be stored easier.

SPELL BOOKS. Photocopy the Spell Books below so that there is one for each player. Spell Books assign players as a specific type of witch or warlock: Hungry, Vain, Deceptive or Necromancer, and each contain 4 spells: some of which will cause harm to specific players, while others will not. Photocopy the Title page and Warning page so there is 1 for each book and staple the Spell Books together.

PLAYING THE GAME

Place the die and all coins in the middle of the board with the cauldron on one side of the board and the spell items on the other. Shuffle the Spell Books and distribute one to each player, as well as a colored stone to use as a game piece.

CHOOSING THE SPELL. The game begins by each player putting a personal item of theirs with the spell items. Personal items may include a watch, earring, ring, etc. Players then look through their book and secretly choose one spell to cast in the game. (However, players may switch spells mid-game.) Each spell requires 7 spell items for casting it, which are written in bold.

AROUND THE BOARD. Each turn, a player rolls the die and moves around the board, starting at the Begin space and moving clockwise. Players will want to gain coins to buy (or steal) spell items for casting their spell. Any time a player rolls a **6**, they get a gold coin, as well as every time they pass the Begin space.

Spaces allow the following actions:
- *Tombstone:* Gain 1 coin
- *Burning Rain of Death:* Lose 1 coin
- *Cat's Eyes:* Take an item from the table without cost
- *Spider Web:* Buy an item from the table or **steal** an item from another player for the correct amount of coins

Players can buy an item from the table for 3 gold coins or *steal* an item from another player for 5 gold coins. Once coins are used, they are placed back in the center of the board. Players can **only** buy items from a spider web space.

CASTING THE SPELLS. When a player has gained all the items they need for their spell, they have won. (However, if a player aims to cast a spell on another player and the spell requires a personal item, the item must be from that particular player.) They then read their spell aloud and place the items into the cauldron. Any actions the spell takes towards another player are carried out.

Once items are put in the cauldron, players may buy them for 5 gold coins each.

THE LAST WITCH OR WARLOCK. The game continues until everyone but the **last** player has completed their spell. This last player loses!

Tips:

- Players should steal spell items whenever possible rather than buying them ... especially if it looks like another player is trying to kill them!
- When taking spell items, choose those that will reveal your spell **last**, such as black skulls or personal items from another player!

MAKE THIS GAME YOUR OWN!

Make your game of Witches and Warlocks *unique by drawing your own mystifying and terrifying pictures on the board. You can also write new spells for future games that can be silly or deadly, such as causing amnesia to force another player to rely on memory alone for casting their spell or causing a plague to kill* all *other players!*

Witches and Warlocks

Object of the Game

Cast your spell and hope to survive your fellow witches and warlocks.

SET UP. Place the die and gold coins in the center of the board with the spell items on one side of the board and the cauldron on the other. Players each get a Spell Book and stone game piece. Players put a personal item of theirs (watch, ring, hair tie, etc.) with the spells items. They then secretly choose a spell from their Spell Book to cast. (However, players may switch spells mid-game.) Each spell requires 7 items which are written in **bold**.

AROUND THE BOARD. Starting at the Begin space, a player rolls the die each turn and moves clockwise around the board to gain or steal coins for spell items. Board spaces do the following:

- *Tombstone:* Gain 1 coin
- *Burning Rain of Death:* Lose 1 coin
- *Cat's Eyes:* Take an item from the table without cost
- *Spider Web:* Buy an item from the table or **steal** an item from another player for the correct amount of coins

COINS are used for the following actions:

- *3 Coins:* Buy a spell item from the table
- *5 Coins:* Steal a spell item from another player **or** buy an item from the cauldron (items from completed spells)
- *Rolling a 6:* Get 1 coin
- *Passing the Begin Space:* Get 1 coin

Players can **only** buy or steal items from a Spider Web space. Coins are returned to the center of the board after buying or stealing items.

CASTING THE SPELL. When a player has all the items they need for their spell, they put the items in the cauldron and read their spell aloud. (If casting a spell on another player and a personal item is required, the item must be from that specific player.) Any action taken against another player is carried out. The player has won and is now out of the game, and the remaining players try to complete their spells.

THE LAST WITCH OR WARLOCK. The last player who never got to complete their spell loses, as well as anyone who was killed.

Spell Book

Witches and Warlocks

HUNGRY WITCH OR WARLOCK

Spell 1: Summoning Children to Eat

"Come little children, I'll take thee away
Into a land of enchantment..."

To summon those who know no wrong,
*Use scent of **rat**, not dead too long,*
*A **personal item** found left around*
*A **stone** and **bone** weighs senses down,*
*An **herb** that bears the name of kin,*
*With a **candle** in **poison** to draw them in.*

Spell 2: Summoning Animals to Eat

*A **bat** or **rat**, whichever comes,*
*A **vial of blood** from previous ones*
Will call them out, both blind and gone
*With a **twig** and **stone** to fall upon.*
*A **candle** and **garlic** bewitches the air*
*With **graveyard dirt** to keep them there.*

Spell 3: Summoning Another Player to Eat

(...and kill out of the game!)

*A **black skull** from a long, lost soul,*
*A **personal item** they wear and show,*
*A bait of **Garlic** is just the trick*
*With a **vial of poison** to kill them quick,*
***Dirt of the graveyard** where fathers lie,*
***Witch Hazel** silences any cries,*
*A **rat** who surely knows the way,*
Will lure them there, and there to stay.

Spell 4: Summoning Another Player to Give You Their Food & Crops

(Player loses a turn as they recover)

Another's treasure you'll surely gain,
*With a **twig** and **stone** found after rain,*
*A **rat** which runs in **graveyard's dirt,***
Make memories that will never hurt.
*A **candle** burns, and **garlic** dims*
The taste of theft and loss within.
***A personal item**, the last you'll need,*
To keep your sense of want and greed.

VAIN WITCH OR WARLOCK

Spell 1: Live Forever
"We want to live forever, not just *until tomorrow."*

> A **candle** as white as the earth is young,
> A dash of **wormwood** under the sun,
> A **stone** around since dawn of time,
> A **twig** that's freshest of its kind,
> **Dirt from the yard** you'll never fill,
> Two drops of **blood** from those who will,
> And last, to remove the pending doubt,
> A drop of **poison** keeps suspicions out.

Spell 2: Make Another Player Idolize You

(Player loses a turn as they recover)

> A **candle** that burns as red as dawn
> Above a **twig** that's short but strong,
> A **vial of blood**, a **stone** inside,
> A **personal item** stripped from their side,
> A dash of **wormwood** and chunk of **bone**
> And the one you choose leaves all they've known.

Spell 3: Kill Another Player

(...Because they get on your nerves!)
"Sweet revenge...!"

> A **skull as black** as the heart that's gone,
> A **candle** to match and **poison** to wrong,
> A **personal item** they surely own,
> A **twig** to stretch and burn with **bone**,
> With a dash of **wormwood**, their end has come,
> And with due course for what they've done.

Spell 4: Make Yourself Look Like Someone Famous

> Burn one **white candle** under the moon,
> That shines its half and hides too soon
> With a drop of **blood** and **twig** to rot,
> With a **stone** and **bone** from a dying lot,
> Add a dash of **garlic** to pierce the air
> And a **personal item** that shows some flair,
> And before the rise of the sun will show
> You'll resemble your chosen from head to toe.

COPY @ 120%

DECEPTIVE WITCH OR WARLOCK

Spell 1: Kill a Player in Their Sleep
(...and out of the game!)

Softly in sleep with spirits weak,
The time comes quickly, dark and sweet.
*A **skull** to shine as black as night,*
*A **candle** to burn its final light,*
*An **herb** to sooth the sullen air,*
*A dash of **poison** to hide in there,*
*A **twig** and **bone** to cross and seal,*
*And a **personal item** for life to steal.*

Spell 2: Make a Player Lose Their Mind
(Player loses a turn as they recover)

*A **personal item** that shows its wear,*
*Drops of **poison** and **blood** to share,*
*A **skull** to burn and turn to flame,*
*A **candle** that puts their mind to shame,*
*An **herb** to daze, a **stone** to weigh,*
Far from themselves, they fly away.

Spell 3: Make a Player Your Slave
(Player loses a turn as they recover)
"I put a spell on you ... and now you're mine!"

A spell to cast in waxing moon,
*With **blood** and **skull**, and ruling soon.*
*A **twig** resembles simpler times,*
*A **stone** crushes the past behind.*
***Two candles** spark and show the way,*
*With a **personal item** they'll come and stay.*

Spell 4: Make a Player Kill Another Player
(First player must choose who they kill!)

Deception's the word,
And power is will;
You choose who you want,
They choose who they kill.
*One **black skull** to bleed,*
*One **white** (skull) to remain,*
*One (personal) **item** is clean,*
*Another (**personal item**) is stained;*
*A **stone** laced with **poison**,*
*And an **herb** to bring out*
The powers that carry
Those with and without.

NECROMANCER WITCH OR WARLOCK

Spell 1: Summon the Dead to Kill Another Player

"Wiggle thy toes, open thine eyes
Twist thy fingers towards the skies..."

*Drizzle the **blood** from killers and worse*
*Upon a **skull** as black as cursed,*
*Top a **bone** of enemy's remains*
*Upon a **stone** of loss and pains,*
*A drop of **poison** with a **twig** beside*
*Is shadowed in **wormwood** in great disguise,*
To call the dead, long lost and quick,
To do this deed: one last, dark trick.

Spell 2: Summon the Dead to Destroy a Village

(2 players lose a turn while they recover)

*A **bone** removed from a forgotten tomb,*
***Dirt** in the night taken under the moon,*
*A **stone** as simple as cause of death,*
*A **twig** as brittle as the final breath,*
*A drop of **blood** from those who escaped,*
*A **personal item** and **herb** for bait,*
And the dead shall rise, to come and extend
Their fate to the towns, and the towns to their end.

Spell 3: Summon the Dead to Use as Slaves

"Damn, damn, double damn!"

To raise the dead for extra hands
With foulest deeds and darkest plans,
*Gather **personal items** (any two) from low and high,*
From some who are dead, and others alive.
*A **bone** that's white, a **stone** that's small,*
*A **rat** that bites, a **twig** that's tall,*
Call them forth with a voice that's strong
*And a drop of **blood** that still runs warm.*

Spell 4: Summon a Demon ... Just to Say Hi

The worlds below are not as far
As timid creatures hope they are.
To summon forth a hellish fiend
For any purpose, any deed,
*Burn one short **candle**, dripping black*
*To burn with **herbs** and **blood** and **bat**,*
*Two drops of **poison** on a **skull** of white*
*With a **bone** to offer in the night.*

COPY @ 120%

Beware of...

Hungry Witches and Warlocks: They use rats!
Vain Witches and Warlocks: They use candles!
Deceptive Witches and Warlocks: They use skulls!
Necromancers: They use bones!

Black skulls ... They mean death to a player!

SECTION III
MODERN HORROR AND SCIENCE FICTION THRILLERS

You've probably noticed that the monster films we know and love today are much different than those we explored in the first section. Death is no longer a clean and neat affair with a simple strangulation and Hollywood scream. It can occur well outside a haunted mansion or moonlit woods, so that you're pretty much screwed no matter where you go. Murders also become much more gruesome and even kids can bite you in the jugular without thinking twice about it. The evolution of make up and intensity of shock value bump these modern movies to a whole new level with monsters that look amazingly realistic, whether they've just risen from the grave or stepped out of your nightmares.

The films in this section include monsters and heroes we love to see both slaughter and triumph — and whichever should occur is just fine. Some of their accompanying games challenge you to jump into the roles of the victims and see if you have what it takes to survive, while others suggest that being the killer isn't all fun and games (though it usually is). You'll find yourself running from Freddy in a killer dream house, trying to exorcise dolls possessed by evil spirits and building a cursed cemetery to raise the dead. Other adventures include trying to survive a circus from hell, keeping a secret journal as a malicious vampire and attempting to shut down a homicidal supercomputer without turning into the undead.

Some scenarios involve standing together with your fellow teammates, while others require saving your own skin and wishing the others good luck. Either way, survival is key, but as the science fiction motto goes: resistance is futile. And by the time the last drop of blood has sprayed, you may find yourself shrugging off that monster movie chase scene at the next midnight showing and think, "Man — I've handled worse."

10
FREDDY'S DREAM HOUSE

Haunted House Survival Game
based on *A Nightmare on Elm Street (1984)*,
6–8 players

A Nightmare on Elm Street stars one of the most famous horror icons in modern culture: Freddy Krueger. We love to hate him, or maybe we just love him, period. He's as funny as he is scary and as demented a killer as we could hope for.

The parents of Elm Street may have taken the law into their own hands to try and free the world of him once and for all, but Freddy found a way to come back and prove he won't

133

be rid of quite so easily. Now left to battle him on their own, the Elm Street children don't stand a chance against either the gloved killer or resisting his domain which we must all succumb to: the dream world.

THE GAME

In this haunted house game, players enter a dream in which they encounter a series of Freddy's killing sprees. If they hope to survive, they must go through each room in the Dream House without being torn to shreds by the lurking killer. But with each turn players face possible mutilation, separation from their friends and getting trapped in the Dream House forever. You will need:

- 50 3 × 5" Index Cards   • 7 Pieces of Red Construction Paper
- 3 Pieces Tan Construction Paper   • Alarm Clock   • Thin, Black Marker
- *A Nightmare on Elm Street* soundtrack

Victim Items: • 4 Pairs of Jeans   • 4 Pairs of Sneakers   • Old, White Sheet
- Pint of Fake Blood

Props: • Noose   • Fake Gun   • Fake Knife   • Pot of Coffee
- Pill Container of Small Candies   • Baseball Cap   • Framed Photo
- Crucifix   • Teddy Bear   • Locket

Additional Items: • CD Burner   • Scissors

Optional Items: • Freddy's Glove   • Freddy's Hat   • Freddy Wall Cling-On

PREPARING THE GAME

To prepare Freddy's Dream House, you'll need to put together the following:
- Invitations   • Game Cards   • Mission Cards   • Trapped Areas
- Props   • Soundtrack Copies   • Death Décor

INVITATIONS. Photocopy the invitations below and send one to each guest. Invitations give a description of the party so that players will know just what kind of bloodbath they're getting themselves into.

GAME CARDS are used to determine what happens to players as they wander through the Dream House. Some cards make Freddy attack or chase players into other rooms while others give them specific instructions to follow. Ninety cards are listed below to be divided into 7 rooms throughout the house. Cards can be made by writing the information onto 4 × 6" plain index cards **cut in half**. Another option is to use printer labels and attach these to index cards. On the back of each card use a thin, red marker to draw 4 long claw marks.

MISSION CARDS. Next, make 10 Mission cards that will give players specific goals to fulfill if they hope to win the game. Mission cards can be made out of 4 × 6" index cards cut in half and should each state one of the following:

- Choose a friend to stay with throughout the game (unless they die). *(2 cards)*
- Take the dead body of your friend Matt out of the dream world.
- Take the dead body of your friend Ralph out of the dream world.
- Take the dead body of your friend Steve out of the dream world.
- Get the Lighter Fluid and Cigarette Lighter card to kill Freddy after 20 minutes.
- Get the Baseball Bat card to kill Freddy after 20 minutes.
- Get the locket that Freddy took to lure you into the Dream House.
- Get the Teddy Bear that Freddy took to lure you into the Dream House.
- Get the framed photo that Freddy took to lure you into the Dream House.

TRAPPED! Each room in the Dream House will also need a Trapped area, which is where players will stand if they become trapped by Freddy. Trapped areas can be made out of a sheet of red construction paper with the word "Trapped" written on it with a black marker. Make 7 Trapped areas so there is one for each room.

DREAM HOUSE PROPS. Sick and demented props will help build a gory atmosphere of the Dream House, as well as provide items players can use in the game:
- *Bloody Gauze:* Players will be getting attacked by Freddy left and right so they'll need some way to show their wounds. Tear an old, faded white sheet into 20 strips and drizzle each strip with fake blood. Let them dry at least 24 hours then divide the strips into the game rooms.
- *Toe Tags:* Some players will also get *killed* by Freddy so they'll need a way to show that they're dead. Make 8 toe tags out of a piece of tan card stock and write "Dead" on each with a thin, black marker. Tie a string around the tags so they can be worn around the neck and divide them in each room.
- *"Real" Weapons:* In this game, anyone could get killed so you'll want a few "real" weapons for players to turn on each other in desperation. "Real" weapons include a fake gun, fake knife and noose to plant in the some of the rooms.

SOUNDTRACK COPIES. Once you've bought or rented the soundtrack to *A Nightmare on Elm Street*, make 1–2 copies so that each floor of the house can play different music from the film.

DEATH DÉCOR. Finally, use the checklist below to turn your house into Freddy's Dream House. Seven rooms are listed to get you started, each of which contains an unfortunate victim that Freddy has already lured in. However, feel free to make any alterations that suit your home. Place the game cards underneath murder victims, sticking out from under the rug, taped to the walls, windows and doors. They should be partially visible and covering several different areas in each room. All cards should be **claw side up.**
　　Living Room: Trapped area, 13 game cards, 3 gauze strips, 2 toe tags
- Pair of sneakers and stuffed pants sticking out from under the couch. Pants sliced up and slightly bloody. "Ralph" card placed on the body with a framed photo beside it.
- Soundtrack playing in the background.
　　Kitchen: Trapped area, 13 game cards, 3 gauze strips, 1 toe tag

- Sneakers and stuffed pants sticking out of a cabinet under the sink, cleaning supplies spilled around it. Bloody baseball cap next to the body with a weapon card underneath it.
- *Counter:* Bottle of sleeping pills (candy in a pill container), coffee pot, mug and spilled coffee grinds.
- *Optional: Freddy's hat on kitchen table.*

Basement: Trapped area, 13 game cards, 3 gauze strips, 1 toe tag

- Sneakers and stuffed pants sticking out from underneath large boxes. "Freddy was here" written in blood on the floor. "Matt" card next to the body with a noose beside it.
- Soundtrack playing in the background.
- *Optional: Freddy's glove on the floor.*

Hallway: Trapped area, 13 game cards, 2 gauze strips, 1 toe tag

- Black garbage bag stuffed with loose clothes. "Steve" written on on a card and taped to bag.

Bathroom: Trapped area, 13 game cards, 3 gauze strips, 1 toe tag

- Bloody, sliced-up towels on the floor and bathtub. Blood smeared on the mirror. Crucifix on a shelf next to a fake knife.

Bedroom: Trapped area, 13 game cards, 3 gauze strips, 1 toe tag

- Stuffed jeans and sweatshirt under a bloody, torn up sheet. A sliced up pillow lies at the foot of the bed. Teddy Bear on the bed and a weapon card under the sheet.
- Timer on the nightstand.
- *Optional: Freddy Pin Up on wall above head of the bed*

Spare Room: Trapped area, 13 game cards, 3 gauze strips, 1 toe tag

- Stuffed sweatshirt, jeans and sneakers on the floor with a small TV where the head should be. A locket next to the body and a fake gun on a bookshelf.
- Soundtrack playing in background.

PLAYING THE GAME

Before the players arrive, play your soundtrack on different floors throughout the Dream House and set each to auto-repeat. Once everyone has arrived, inform the players they are about to fall asleep and enter Freddy's Dream House. Once asleep, they will have 20 minutes to stay alive and fulfill a specific mission until bringing Freddy out of the dream world to destroy him once and for all.

BEGINNING THE GAME. The game begins by each player choosing a Mission card. Players may reveal their mission to the others, but are not required to. Everyone then splits up into the bedroom and spare room. The timer is set for 20 minutes and each player chooses one card from around the room for their first turn.

FOLLOWING THE CARDS. Players must do what is instructed on their card:

- *Chased:* If the card says that Freddy has chased them into another room, they **must** go to that room to pick up their next card.

- *Slashed:* If the card says the player has been slashed by Freddy, they must take one of the bloody bandages and wrap it around the area where they were attacked. **3 slashes from Freddy mean death.**
- *Weapons:* Weapon cards can be used to fight off Freddy **once**. Weapon cards can also be given to another player, but can only stop future attacks, not past ones.
- *Instructions:* The player must fulfill the instructions on their card before taking their next card.

With each turn, players must go to a new room to take their next card unless their current game card states otherwise. Players choose only one card per turn, and unless chased, should go into a room where at least one card remains. Players all take their turns together, and not one at a time. Once players read their cards they should keep them in their pocket so they do not accidentally get reused. Any cards that can be used in future turns should be kept on the top of their card pile. However, Weapon cards must be kept visible in their hand.

WEAPONS. When a player gets a weapon card they cannot hide it in their pocket. Rather, they must keep it in their hand throughout the game. After using a weapon card to ward off getting slashed by Freddy, the player must leave the card **face up** in the room it was used. The weapon card can now be taken by another player. (Taking a face-up weapon card counts as a turn.) If a player is given a weapon card by another player, they do not need to follow any additional instructions on it.

The 3 "real" weapons in the Dream House (the noose, gun and knife) cannot be used to stop Freddy. However, they can be used against other players. Players can only take a "real" weapon if they have a card that tells them to do so.

GETTING TRAPPED. If a player goes into a room and there are no more cards in it, they must stand on the Trapped area, as they are now trapped by Freddy. If someone is already on the trapped area in that room, the player who is *not* on the Trapped area **dies**. If they have to find a card in a certain **location** in any room (ex: *Your next card must be from a wall*) and there are no cards in that location in any room, they are confined to a Trapped area of any room.

The only way to get free from being trapped is if another player gets a *Saved Someone Trapped* card for that particular room. The player with the card can save them before going to a different room to take their turn. If a person is alone on a particular floor when they get trapped, they should yell to other players that they are trapped. Anyone still trapped when 20 minutes is up dies.

MISSIONS. Throughout the game, players will want to fulfill their mission. However, if their mission requires taking a specific item, they can only take the item when they are taking a turn in that room. If a player sees that someone else has the item they need to fulfill their mission, they may ask them for it but cannot take it by force.

DEAD PLAYERS. When a player is killed, they must leave any weapon cards or *Save Someone Trapped* cards they are holding face up in whatever room they were killed. The dead player must then take a toe tag and wear it around their neck for the remainder of the game. After a player dies they must follow a *living* player around for the remainder of the game, either sticking with the same person or following different people each turn. They can no longer take cards, but are allowed to read cards that have not yet been played and try to convince living players to take them, either to help them (as friendly spirits) or try to kill them (being possessed by Freddy). If everyone dies in the game except for one player **or** only one player is left that has not been trapped, that player cannot get trapped, but must go through the remainder of the rooms to try and finish off all the cards without getting killed.

THE TIMER. When the timer goes off after 20 minutes, Freddy has come out of the dream with the players. However, if any game cards were not played, it means that Freddy is still in the dream world and did not come out to be destroyed. If anyone picks up a "Freddy slashes you" card exactly when the timer goes off, Freddy comes out of the dream with them and kills them unless they have a weapon or someone gives them one.

WINNING THE GAME. In order to win the game, players must do each of the following:
- Stay alive for 20 minutes,
- Have fulfilled their mission,
- Not be trapped when the timer goes off,
- At least 1 player must be holding a weapon card, and
- All of the cards in the Dream House must be played.

Tips:
- This is a timed game, so even when players have to wrap themselves in gauze, they should hustle!
- When using fake blood, keep in mind that it will not stain clothes or the bathroom mirror. However, it *can* stain white walls!

MAKE THIS GAME YOUR OWN!

Set up the murder scenes in the Dream House any way you like, such as using weapons, chains or any other assortment of props. You can also make new game cards and Mission cards for future games to give players new obstacles to overcome.

LIKE THIS GAME?

Check out The Nightly Haunt *in Chapter 5 for another Haunted House game!*

Freddy's Dream House

Object of the Game

Survive and fulfill your mission in Freddy's Dream House
to pull him out of the dream world and destroy him once and for all.

STARTING THE GAME. Each player is given a Mission card. Players split up into the bedroom and spare room and the timer is set for 20 minutes. Each player chooses their first card.

CARDS

- *Chased by Freddy:* Player **must** go to where they are chased to pick up their next card. Players who have not been chased may go to any new room next turn.
- *Slashed by Freddy:* Player must take a bloody bandage and wrap it around the area where they were slashed. **3 slashes from Freddy mean death.**
- *Weapon Cards:* Used to fight off Freddy once on a future turn. Can also be given to another player.
- *Instructions:* Player must fulfill the instructions on their card before taking their next one.

All players take turns at once, and not one at a time. Each turn they must go into a new room unless their current card states otherwise. Players take one card per turn and, unless chased, should go to a room where at least one card remains. After using their card, players put it in their pocket (unless it is a weapon) so it does not get reused. Cards that may be used in future turns should be kept on the top of their card pile.

WEAPONS. Weapon cards are not kept in a player's pocket but must remain in their hand until used. After using a weapon card, it is put **face up** in the room it was used for another player to take. Taking a face-up weapon card counts as a turn. The 3 "real" weapons (noose, gun and knife) cannot be used to stop Freddy. However, they can be used against other players. Players can only take a "real" weapon if they have a card that tells them to do so.

TRAPPED! If a player goes into a room and there are no more cards in it, they must stand in the Trapped area, as they are now trapped by Freddy. If someone is already on the trapped area, the player standing outside it **dies**. If a player must find a card in a certain location (*Ex: Your next card must be from under a rug*) and there are no cards in that location in any room, they are trapped in any room they choose.

Players can only get free from being trapped if another player gets a *Save Someone Trapped* card for that particular room. The player with the card can get them out before going to a different room to take their turn. If a person is alone on a particular floor when they get trapped, they should yell to other players to get their attention. **Anyone trapped after 20 minutes dies.**

MISSIONS. Players must fulfill their mission if they hope to win the game. However, if their mission requires taking a specific item, they can only take the item when they are taking their turn in that particular room. If a player sees that someone else has the item they need to fulfill their mission, they may ask them for it but cannot take it by force.

DEAD PLAYERS. When a player is killed, they must drop any weapon cards and *Save Someone Trapped* cards they are holding and put them face up in the room where they were killed. They then take a toe tag and wear it around their neck.

Dead players must follow a living person for the remainder of the game, either the same person or switching each turn. Dead players may look at unused cards and try to persuade living players to take them, either to help them or get them killed. If everyone dies in the game except for one player **or** only one player is left that has not been trapped, that player cannot get trapped but must go through the remainder of the rooms to try and finish off all the cards without getting killed.

WHEN TIME IS UP. When the timer goes off after 20 minutes, Freddy has come out of the dream. However, if any game cards were not played it means Freddy is still in the dream world and did not come out to be destroyed. If anyone picks up a "Freddy attacks" card exactly when the timer goes off, Freddy comes out of the dream with them and kills them unless they have a weapon or someone gives them one.

WINNING THE GAME. In order to win the game, players must do each of the following:

- Stay alive for 20 minutes
- Have fulfilled their mission
- Not be trapped when the timer goes off
- At least 1 player must be holding a weapon card to kill Freddy
- All of the cards in the Dream House must be played.

You are invited to the bloodiest survival game:

Freddy's Dream House

based on Wes Craven's *A Nightmare on Elm Street*

Come venture on the mission of bringing Freddy out of the dream world to finish him off once and for all. But be warned ... along the way you'll witness his bloodiest work first-hand, meet some of his most recent victims and possibly become trapped in the dream world forever.

Freddy's Haunted House Survival Game

Date:

Time:

Location:

Please RSVP.

Until then...

Whatever you do: **Don't Fall Asleep.**

Game Cards

2 of each:
- Freddy **slashes you** and chases you into the kitchen.
- Freddy **slashes you** and chases you into the master bedroom.
- Freddy **slashes you** and chases you into the spare bedroom.
- Freddy **slashes you** and chases you into the hallway.
- Freddy **slashes you** and chases you into the cellar.
- Freddy **slashes you** and chases you into the bathroom.
- Freddy **slashes you** and chases you into the living room.
- You hide from Freddy under the rug. Your next card must be under a rug.
- Freddy starts to come out of the wall to scare you. Your next card must be from a wall.
- Freddy chases you to a window. Your next card must be from a window.
- Freddy chases you into a door. Your next card must be from a door.
- You start to feel yourself waking up. Take a "sleeping pill" before your next card.
- You know that one of your dead friends (bodies) in the Dream House had a weapon. Search the bodies to find it next turn.
- You hide from Freddy behind another player. Follow someone next turn.
- Freddy slams the door. You must stay in this room for your next turn.

1 of each:
- Freddy chases you into the kitchen.
- Freddy chases you into the master bedroom.
- Freddy chases you into the spare bedroom.
- Freddy chases you into the hallway.
- Freddy chases you into the cellar.
- Freddy chases you into the bathroom.
- Freddy chases you into the living room.
- Freddy **slashes** your shoulder.
- Freddy **slashes** your face.
- Freddy **slashes** your stomach.
- Freddy **slashes** your ear.
- Freddy **slashes** your hand.
- Freddy sees that weapon you're holding and snatches it! If you have a weapon card, drop it and leave it (face up).
- If you see a player who has not been slashed, follow them for protection until they *do* get slashed.
- Freddy knocks you unconscious. You stay in this room next turn while your head clears.
- You're losing blood fast... If you've been slashed, it counts as double.
- You've injured yourself in a panic and can no longer move without help. Depend on another player to help you walk or else crawl into rooms alone.
- Find a "real" weapon around the house: a knife, gun or noose. If anyone tries to steal a weapon card from you, kill them with it.

- You're starting to panic. Each time you see a dead player, scream in terror.
- You accidentally step on a dead person. If you're holding a weapon card, you drop it and leave it (face up) in a panic.
- You think Freddy is after a friend of yours. Stick with them next turn.
- You think Freddy will leave you alone if you abandon the others. Go to the next room *alone.*
- If you are carrying anything, give it to a dead player to carry for you for the remainder of the game.
- If you see someone trapped and you can't save them, stick a dead player with them.
- You start to panic. If another player has a weapon card, take it from them.
- You're desperate to get out of the Dream House. Take all your future cards from windows until there are none left.
- You're desperate to get out of the Dream House. Take all your future cards from doors until there are none left.
- If you are followed by a dead person, put on any bloody bandages they wear, as they have bled all over you. (These do not count as slashes from Freddy.)
- Refuse to touch a dead body. You cannot take a card next to a dead body unless a future card instructs you to.
- You've run into another player's weapon in a panic. Put on a bandage that counts as a slash from Freddy if anyone in the room has a weapon.
- You help protect a friend from Freddy. If any other player got slashed in this room *this turn*, you get the bandage instead.
- Take the "real" gun to steal a weapon card from another player on a future turn.
- Take the "real" noose to steal a weapon card from another player on a future turn.
- Find the baseball cap from your dead best friend, then take your next card.
- Take the picture of your dead best friend, then take your next card.
- Find a dead body. Carry it with you for the remainder of the game as a safety shield, as it will protect you from one future attack.
- Look for a face-up weapon card in any room. If you can't find one, follow another player each turn until you do. (Continue to take a card each turn.)
- Keep tabs on the time remaining until everyone wakes up. As each minute goes by, announce how much time is left.
- If you see any cleaning supplies around the house, take a bottle to hold as a security blanket.
- If at any point you have 2 slash marks, go to a Trapped area until someone saves you. Lose 1 slash while you wait.
- If you find that someone has been killed by a TV, turn on the TV in shock and watch it. Don't take your next turn until someone else comes in the room.
- Find a sliced up pillow. Keep it with you as a security blanket, as it will prevent one future slash from Freddy.
- Find a bloody towel. Put it over a dead body to give them their dignity.
- Find a dead player to take with you on your next 2 turns. The dead player takes your cards for you, so that any possible slashes don't affect you.
- If most of the players are dead, take your turns in separate rooms from the others if possible.

- Look for a "real" weapon throughout the house. In each room where there isn't one, scream "Noooo!"
- Find a place where Freddy has written a message and take your next card from that room. Convince another player to go with you.
- *Weapon:* Lighter Fluid and Cigarette Lighter. You don't want anyone to see you have this yet. Next turn, hide so that no one sees you, but take your next card.
- *Weapon:* Butcher Knife. If there are any players who have been slashed twice (not including you), give them this card.
- *Weapon:* Sledgehammer. If you have not been slashed, give this to a player who has.
- *Weapon:* Pool Cue. If any player is Trapped, go to a room nearby so they can see or hear you.
- *Weapon:* Baseball Bat. Get a drink of coffee before your next card.
- *Weapon:* Cricket Bat. Carry the coffee can for the remainder of the game.
- **Save Someone Trapped:** Master Bedroom. Take and keep the bottle of sleeping pills. Give players pills only if they need them.
- **Save Someone Trapped:** Spare Bedroom. If you see another player carrying a dead body, help them for the remainder of the game unless a new card instructs otherwise.
- **Save Someone Trapped:** Bathroom. Avoid going into the bathroom. If you must, make a loud vomiting sound, as you're totally grossed out.
- **Save Someone Trapped:** Hallway. If a player has been trapped in the hallway, bring a dead body to take their place and fool Freddy.
- **Save Someone Trapped:** Living Room. Take the crucifix as a security blanket, then take your next card.
- **Save Someone Trapped:** Kitchen. If a dead player follows you, tie a bloody bandage over their eyes.
- **Save Someone Trapped:** Basement. If you see a dead player, convince them to follow you to where someone is trapped. The dead player takes the trapped player's place.

11
DOLLS FROM HELL

Spell Casting and Doll Mutilation Game
based on *Child's Play (1988)*,
3–6 players

Some people are afraid of clowns. Some people are afraid of dogs. After *Child's Play*, we were *all* afraid of dolls. *Child's Play* proposed that the urban legends you hear about possessed and demonic dolls may not be mere stories after all, and it's just not worth taking the risk either way. These dolls may be found at dark and shady occult shops, on display at your local toy store ... or just maybe there are a few in your own home, right now.

145

THE GAME

In this game, players take on the roles of demon hunters facing an army of possessed dolls. Their mission: to destroy every last one and vanquish their souls straight to hell, including the ultimate doll of evil: Chucky himself! The game room is set up to look like a back alley toy store with dolls, stuffed animals and action figures lining the walls and dressed to kill. They may be made of stuff and fluff, but these possessed toys won't be taken down too easily, as each must be killed with specific spells and weapons, and choosing incorrectly could mean your life. You will need:

- 30 Dolls, Action Figures or Stuffed Animals   • 30 4 × 6" Plain Index Cards
- 30 Paper Clips   • Small Journal or Sketch Pad   • Pen **for each Player**
Weapons: • 3 Colored Gem Stones   • Vial of Holy Water (Plain Water)
- Blade   • Candle   • Crucifix   • Scissors   • Fake Gun
- Vial of Acid (Watered down Cola)   • Pentagram   • "Blessed" Cloth
Additional Supplies: • Scissors   • Double-Sided Tape
Optional Item: • Chucky Doll

PREPARING THE GAME

To make *Dolls from Hell*, you'll need to put together the following:
- Killer Dolls   • Doll Cards   • Game Sheets   • Spell Book

KILLER DOLLS. You'll want a total of 30 dolls for your possessed toy store: 26 of which will be evil, 3 will be safe and 1 will be Chucky. If you don't have a Chucky doll, you can alter any kind of doll to resemble him with wild red hair and scars on his face. You can also use other sorts of toys for the army of evil dolls, such as stuffed animals, puppets, action figures, and other toys that look like they could come to life any minute and wipe out the neighborhood. If your current count of homicidal dolls is less than 30, pick up a few at your local second hand shop or tag sales.

Throughout the game, it will be unknown which dolls are evil and which are safe, but to spice up the horror of it all, make them *all* look demented in their own way. Mess up their hair, paint their eyes red, black or white, put bloody bandages around them or paint bruises on their face.

DOLL CARDS. Next, photocopy the Evil Dolls and How to Kill the Dolls pages below, then cut and tape each onto a 4 × 6" blank index card **cut in half**. These cards will assign the dolls as either safe or evil, and as specific types of killers. Clip the pairs of cards together with a paperclip, putting the Evil Doll card on top and the How to Kill the Doll card underneath it. Dolls that are not evil will have a blank card as their second card. All together you'll have the following pairs:

26 pairs:
- Evil Doll (states how the doll kills people, points given and time limit for killing it)
- How to Kill the Doll (states weapon and spell needed to destroy the doll)

3 pairs:
- Doll is not Evil (doll gives no points and does not harm the player)
- (Blank card)

GAME SHEETS. Photocopy the Weapons and How to use Them sheet to help identify dolls as those possessed by spirits or people. Photocopy a Score Sheet so you have one for each player to keep track of points throughout the game.

SPELL BOOK. The last item you'll need is the Spell Book, which contains spells needed to vanquish the spirits of the dolls straight to hell. To make the book, write or photocopy the spells below and put them into a small, blank journal. Separate the Spell Book into 2 sections: Demonic Spirits and Human Spirits. Each spell works to kill at least one doll, either possessed by a demon or a person before they died. Finally, make a cover page that says "*Spell Book for Possessed Dolls.*"

PLAYING THE GAME

To set up the game, place the dolls all around the room on shelves, tables, furniture, and along the floor. Without looking at the cards, place a pair **face down** underneath each doll. (This way you won't know which dolls are evil and which are safe.) The only doll that does not need a pair of cards is Chucky, who is evil in every way. Place the weapons and the Spell Book on a small table along with the Weapons and How to Use Them sheet.

IN THE EVIL SHOP. Players are each given a Score Sheet and pen. Each turn, a player chooses a doll and tries to destroy it. This is done by looking at the doll's **top card** to see if it is evil or not. If the doll is not evil, no points are awarded and the turn is over. If the doll is evil, the player gives the bottom card (How to Kill the Doll) to **one** other player. They must now try to figure out how to kill the doll in the time stated.

KILLING THE DOLL. To kill the doll, the player must use each of the weapons to see which one is required to kill it. For each weapon they try, they lose 10 minutes of time, which they mark on their Score Sheet. The player who holds the How to Kill the Doll card tells them when they have chosen the correct weapon, but only after they have used it on the doll.

Weapons are used as follows:
- Holy Water: *Sprinkle over doll (Demonic)* • *Candle:* Hold above doll (Demonic)
- *Crucifix:* Lay over doll (Demonic) • *Magic stones:* Place on doll (Demonic)
- *Pentagram:* Lay over doll (Demonic) • *Blessed Cloth:* Drape over doll (Demonic)
- *Blade:* Cut doll (Human) • *Scissors:* Cut doll (Human)
- *Gun:* Shoot doll (Human) • *Acid:* Sprinkle over doll (Human)

(As the creator of the game, it is up to you whether you truly want the dolls to be cut or if players should just pretend to cut them!)

VANQUISHING THE EVIL SPIRIT. Once the doll is killed, the player must find the correct spell to vanquish its spirit so that it cannot come back again. The specific weapon that killed the doll will be a clue of which type of spell is needed. If the weapon was one that kills demonic dolls, the player should read the spells that cast out demonic spirits. If the weapon was one for killing dolls possessed by people, the player should read those spells.

Players try out the spells by looking through the spell book and reading them aloud. For each spell read, the player loses 15 seconds. The player also receives 1 strike from the doll for each incorrect spell recited, as the doll is slowly coming back to life. Six strikes means the doll has beaten the player unconscious and their turn is over. The player holding the How to Kill the Doll card announces when the correct spell is being cast, but only after the second line of the spell has been read. The player must find and read the correct spell in the allotted time in order to destroy the doll for good. Killing a doll earns the number of points shown on the doll's card. Failure to destroy the doll makes the player lose 1 point.

DOLLS THAT WON'T DIE. If the doll does not get destroyed, it stays in the game to be tried again, but cannot be attempted by the player who held the How to Kill the Doll card. Each time the doll is again attempted but not destroyed, the **original player who chose it** loses a point, as does the one who tried to destroy it the second time. After each turn, players add up how many strikes they have been dealt by the doll and mark how many points they are awarded if they successfully destroyed it. If at any time a player has -5 points or less, they have been killed by the possessed dolls.

BATTLING CHUCKY. Players need a total of 15 points to battle Chucky. Once they have the necessary points, two **other** players decide what will kill him, one choosing a weapon and the other the spell. Both the weapon and spell can be for battling either demonic spirits **or** human spirits. Players mark their choices on the bottom of their Score Sheets. The player to battle Chucky then tries the different weapons and spells until the correct ones are chosen. Incorrect weapons and spells use the same amount of time as on the other dolls. Failure to destroy Chucky makes the player lose **5 points.** Each time a player battles Chucky, two players choose a new weapon and spell that destroy him.

WINNING THE GAME. The game continues until either:
- A player successfully destroys Chucky,
- All of the dolls (except Chucky) have been destroyed, and the one with the most points wins, or
- All players are dead but one.

MAKE THIS GAME YOUR OWN!

Make your version of Dolls from Hell *all your own by decking out your assortment of possessed dolls horror-movie style. Spray them with fake blood, tear their clothes, give them scars and rip off a few body parts.*

You can also write your own spells for the Spell Book and alter the ways the dolls kill the players — particularly if some of your guests have phobias that you can incorporate into the game.

Dolls from Hell

Object of the Game

Destroy as many possessed dolls as you can
to finally vanquish the infamous Chucky.

Destructive dolls are placed throughout the game room. The Spell Book, weapons and Weapon sheet are put on the game table. Each player is given a Score sheet and pen.

EACH TURN. One player chooses a doll and looks at its top card (Evil Doll), giving the bottom card (How to Kill the Doll) to one other player. If the doll is not evil, no points are awarded and the turn is over. If the doll is evil, the player must figure out how to kill it in the allotted time.

KILLING THE DOLL. The player tries each weapon on the doll until discovering the one that kills it. Each weapon uses 10 seconds, which the player marks on their Score sheet. The player holding the How to Kill the Doll card announces when the correct weapon has been used.

VANQUISHING THE SPIRIT. The player must then find the correct spell from the Spell Book to vanquish the spirit of the doll. Each spell uses 15 seconds, and each incorrect spell makes the doll strike as it regains its strength. The first 2 lines of the spell must be read aloud before the card holder announces it is correct. The spell must be read in its entirety before the allotted time runs out. Killing a doll earns the number of points on the doll's card. Failure to destroy the doll makes the player lose 1 point.

DOLLS THAT WON'T DIE. If the player is dealt a total of 6 strikes on a turn, the doll has beaten them unconscious and the turn is over. The doll stays in the game to be tried again. However, the player who originally looked at the How to Kill the Doll card cannot try to destroy it. Each time the doll is again attempted but not destroyed **the original player who chose it** loses a point, as does the one who tried to destroy it a second time. If at any time a player has -5 points or less, they have been killed by the possessed dolls.

BATTLING CHUCKY. Players need a total of 15 points to battle Chucky. When they do this, two other players chose a weapon and spell, writing one or the other on the bottom of their Score sheets. Weapons and spells can be for either demonic spirits or human spirits. The player battles Chucky in the same fashion as other dolls with each incorrect item and spell using the same amount of time. Each time a player battles Chucky, two players chose a new weapon and spell that destroy him. Failure to destroy Chucky makes the player lose 5 points.

WINNING THE GAME. The game continues until either:
- A player successfully destroys Chucky,
- All of the dolls (except Chucky) have been destroyed and the one with the most points wins, *or*
- All players are dead but one.

Evil Doll Cards

EVIL DOLL

Causes Heart Attack

3 points

Kill Time: 2 minutes

EVIL DOLL

Chokes Player

4 points

Kill Time: 1.5 minutes

EVIL DOLL

Causes Internal Bleeding

3 points

Kill Time: 2 minutes

EVIL DOLL

Causes Player's Head to Explode

4 points

Kill Time: 1.5 minutes

EVIL DOLL

Locks Player in the Fridge

3 points

Kill Time: 3 minutes

EVIL DOLL

Throws Player off a Building

3 points

Kill Time: 3 minutes

EVIL DOLL

Throws Player in Traffic

4 points

Kill Time: 2 minutes

EVIL DOLL

Bashes Player's Head into the Wall

4 points

Kill Time: 2.5 minutes

EVIL DOLL

Causes Fatal Car Accident

3 points

Kill Time: 2 minutes

EVIL DOLL

Scares Player to Death

5 points

Kill Time: 1.5 minutes

EVIL DOLL

Smashes Player in Face with Shovel

4 points

Kill Time: 2 minutes

EVIL DOLL

Gouges out Player's Eyes

5 points

Kill Time: 1.5 minutes

EVIL DOLL

Blows up the Building

5 points

Kill Time: 1.5 minutes

EVIL DOLL

Throws Player into Acid

5 points

Kill Time: 1.5 minutes

COPY @ 120%

EVIL DOLL

Stabs Player with a Butcher Knife

4 points

Kill Time: 2 minutes

EVIL DOLL

Throws Player into a Chipper

4 points

Kill Time: 3 minutes

EVIL DOLL

Tears Player's Arms Off

5 points

Kill Time: 1.5 minutes

EVIL DOLL

Strangles Player

4 points

Kill Time: 2 minutes

EVIL DOLL

Bashes Player's Head
in with a Hammer

4 points

Kill Time: 2 minutes

EVIL DOLL

Chops up Player with an Axe

3 points

Kill Time: 3 minutes

DOLL NOT EVIL

DOLL NOT EVIL

EVIL DOLL

Injects Player with Cleaning Fluid

4 points

Kill Time: 1.5 minutes

EVIL DOLL

Bites Player to Death

4 points

Kill Time: 2.5 minutes

EVIL DOLL

Pushes a Bookcase onto Player

3 points

Kill Time: 2.5 minutes

EVIL DOLL

Throws Player into the Oven

5 points

Kill Time: 2 minutes

EVIL DOLL

Injects Player with Poison

3 points

Kill Time: 2.5 minutes

EVIL DOLL

Uses an Electric Nail Gun on Player

3 points

Kill Time: 2.5 minutes

DOLL NOT EVIL

How to Kill the Doll Cards

Weapon:

Holy Water

Spell:

I bid you, dark entity
Be gone and never return
I remove from this doll
The weight of evil, the power of darkness

Weapon:

Holy Water

Spell:

This demon of old
Dark creature of age
You are removed from your keeper
And stripped of this world

Weapon:

Holy Water

Spell:

In the name of all that is good
And contains light
Strip away the hidden darkness
That lingers within

Weapon:

Candle

Spell:

Unknown demon
Journey back to the torment that awaits
A hundred fold greater
Than all you have done

Weapon:

Candle

Spell:

Damnation, return
To the hole whence you came
I remove the black fire
And leave nothing but ash

Weapon:

Crucifix

Spell:

This demon of old
Dark creature of age
You are removed from your keeper
And stripped of this world

Weapon:

Crucifix

Spell:

Ruler of the deep,
You are expelled from your shell
The power to heal has overcome you
Powerless now and defeated

Weapon:

Magic Stones

Spell:

In the name of all that is good
And contains light
Strip away the hidden darkness
That lingers within

Weapon:

Blessed Cloth

Spell:

Ruler of the deep,
You are expelled from your shell
The power to heal has overcome you
Powerless now and defeated

Weapon:

Pentagram

Spell:

Evil spirit now here residing,
I cast you out
Back to the depths of hell
Which you sought to escape

COPY @ 120%

COPY @ 120%

Weapon:

Magic Stones

Spell:

Evil doer
Of torment and death
I remove you from this binding
To enter eternal binds below

Weapon:

Blessed Cloth

Spell:

Damnation, return
To the hole whence you came
I remove the black fire
And leave nothing but ash

Weapon:

Candle

Spell:

Evil doer
Of torment and death
I remove you from this binding
To enter eternal binds below

Weapon:

Crucifix

Spell:

Unknown demon
Journey back to the torment that awaits
A hundred fold greater
Than all you have done

Weapon:

Acid

Spell:

Trapped spirit, broken soul,
Your time has ended
The curse is broken
And its evil is lost

Weapon:

Gun

Spell:

Spirits of light, remove from this doll
What has unrightfully entered
And send it back
From whence it came

Weapon:

Acid

Spell:

Trapped spirit, broken soul,
Your time has ended
The curse is broken
And its evil is lost

Weapon:

Scissors

Spell:

Spirit that lingers,
Your name is forgotten
And your soul destroyed
Enter the darker realm that awaits you

Weapon:

Gun

Spell:

Spirits of light, remove from this doll
What has unrightfully entered
And send it back
From whence it came

Weapon:

Scissors

Spell:

Unknown mortal,
Immortally unbound
Pass into the beyond
Leaving your horrid deeds behind

Weapon:

Blade

Spell:

Unknown mortal,
Immortally bound
Pass into the beyond
Leaving your horrid deeds behind

Weapon:

Acid

Spell:

Robber of Light
May the misery be returned to you
That you have caused or tried to cause
In destructive ways

Weapon:

Pentagram

Spell:

Evil spirit now here residing,
I cast you out
Back to the depths of hell
Which you sought to escape

Weapon:

Blade

Spell:

Robber of Light
May the misery be returned to you
That you have caused or tried to cause
In destructive ways

Weapon:

Blade

Spell:

Wrongful doer
Hidden with secret
You are removed and destroyed
By the power of light

Weapon:

Gun

Spell:

Divine spirits
Remove the soul from this object
Break the binds that hold it here
And send it back into infinity

COPY @ 120%

Weapons and How to Use Them

Each uses 10 seconds

Dolls Possessed by Demons

Holy Water: Sprinkle over doll
Candle: Hold above doll
Crucifix: Lay over doll
Pentagram: Lay over doll
Blessed Sheet: Drape over doll
Magic Stones: Place on doll

Dolls Possessed by Human Spirits

Blade: Cut doll
Scissors: Cut doll
Gun: Shoot doll
Acid: Sprinkle over doll

Dolls from Hell
Score Sheet

Battling Dolls   Points
Time Lost: Strikes:

Chucky's Weapon & Spell

Spell Book for Possessed Dolls

Demonic Spirits

I bid you, dark entity
Be gone and never return
I remove from this doll
The weight of evil, the power of darkness

In the name of all that is good
And contains light
Strip away the hidden darkness
That lingers within

Evil spirit now here residing,
I cast you out
Back to the depths of hell
Which you sought to escape

Unknown demon
Journey back to the torment that awaits
A hundred fold greater
Than all you have done

Damnation, return
To the hole whence you came
I remove the black fire
And leave nothing but ash
Ruler of the deep,
You are expelled from your shell
The power to heal has overcome you
Powerless now and defeated

This demon of old
Dark creature of age
You are removed from your keeper
And stripped of this world

Evil doer
Of torment and death
I remove you from this binding
To enter eternal binds below

Human Spirits

Divine spirits
Remove the soul from this object
Break the binds that hold it here
And send it back into infinity

Spirits of light, remove from this doll
What has unrightfully entered
And send it back
From whence it came

Robber of Light
May the misery be returned to you
That you have caused or tried to cause
In destructive ways

Unknown mortal,
Immortally bound
Pass into the beyond
Leaving your horrid deeds behind

Spirit that lingers,
Your name is forgotten
And your soul destroyed
Enter the darker realm that awaits you

Trapped spirit, broken soul,
Your time has ended
The curse is broken
And its evil is lost

Wrongful doer
Hidden with secret
You are removed and destroyed
By the power of light

12

WHERE THE DEAD WALK

Cursed Graveyard Board Game
based on *Pet Sematary (1989)*,
2–6 players

Stephen King's *Pet Sematary* just goes to show that when you decide to pick up and move, *anything* can happen. To stay on the safe side, it's best to avoid houses on New England country roads with hidden cemeteries just down the path.

Pet Sematary actually presents us with two creepy cemeteries, each one sinister in its own right. The ancient Indian burial ground appears evil even before we learn about the dark magic it contains, and the Pet Sematary itself is an ominous yet innocent creation put together by the hands of children. One may be safe, but the other lies beyond a barrier not meant to be crossed, lest a certain succession of death should keep you ever crawling back.

THE GAME

In this board game, players make graves in the sour soil of the Mick Mack burial ground for all the wrong reasons. Burying those who have suffered a recent demise, they know fully well that what comes back will be purely evil in nature. But once the ground is broken, there's no turning back ... and with each stone unturned players risk their *own* lives in the ground where the dead walk. You will need:

- 108 Small Stones • 2 Sheets of Brown Card Stock
- Sheet of Black Poster Board • Gray and Red 3-D Paint
- White-Out Pen • Scissors

PREPARING THE GAME

To make the game, you'll need to put together the following:
- Game Board • Remains Cards • Cursed Stones

THE BOARD. To make the board for the game, cut out a 17 × 20" piece of black poster board. Following the model below, use gray 3-D paint to draw a small circle in the center of the board with 2 larger circles around it. In the smallest circle make 5 large dots to represent burial mounds. Draw 7 dots in the center circle and 6 dots in the outer circle. Around the parameter of either side of the outer circle write "Where the Dead Walk" with gray and red paint. For extra support you can also use double-sided tape to apply the board to a sheet of plywood so that it doesn't warp and it can be stored easier.

REMAINS CARDS. To make the Remains cards, cut out 18 2 × 2" squares out of brown cardstock. Use a White-Out pen to draw or write the following on the back of each:
- 6 Hands • 4 White Skulls • 3 Bones
- 3 Blank (nothing written or drawn) • 2 Black Skulls

CURSED STONES. Finally, paint a black dot on the bottom of 18 small stones to use as "cursed" stones in the game.

PLAYING THE GAME

To set up the game, shuffle the Remains cards and place one **face down** on each mound (dot) on the board, then top with 1 stone. Line the remaining stones around the parameter of the board, keeping any black marks face down.

BUILDING THE MOUNDS. Players will want to build as many grave mounds in the cemetery as they can without getting killed in the process. Each turn, a player places 1 stone on any mound. If they pick up a cursed stone they lose their turn and the cursed stone is tossed aside. Players may build onto **any** mound, including those other players have started. Once 5 stones are on a mound, it is complete.

UNEARTHING THE MOUNDS. When a player puts the fifth stone on a mound and completes the grave, they may flip over the Remains card underneath it. However, players are not required to do this, and may leave the mound for another player to unearth.

The following outcomes occur when unearthing a grave:

- *Blank:* The dead does not return. Player is not affected.
- *Hand:* The dead has risen to kill another player out of the game. If a player unearths 2 hands, they decide who gets killed. (Each hand can only be used once.)
- *White Skull:* The dead has risen, tried to attack and failed. If a player digs up 2 white skulls over the course of the game, they die.
- *Black Skull:* The site is cursed by an evil force. The dead has risen and killed the player out of the game.
- *Bone:* The dead has risen and wandered off aimlessly. Once 2 bones have been dug up, cursed stones **kill** players who pick them up.

Once unearthed, players keep Remains cards in front of them. Once all the mounds have been completed with 5 stones, players **must** unearth a mound each turn.

WINNING THE GAME. The game ends when only one player is left alive.

MAKE THIS GAME YOUR OWN!

Make your version of Where the Dead Walk *unique in the way you choose to design the board. Draw a series of evil images between the mounds, such as ghastly trees, half-exposed skulls or shovels. You can also use skull and bones stickers when making the Remains cards.*

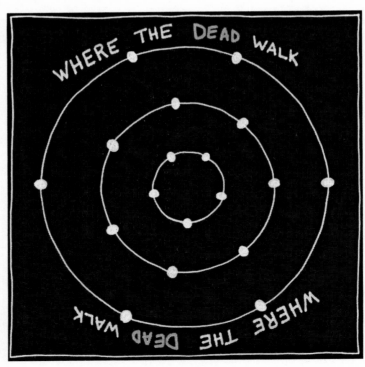

Where the Dead Walk

Object of the Game

Try and survive the cursed grounds while bringing the dead back to life.

SET UP. Place a Remains card **face down** on each mound (dot) on the board with 1 stone on top of it. Remaining stones are placed around the parameter of the board with any black marks kept face down.

BUILDING THE MOUNDS. Each turn, a player takes 1 stone from the parameter of the board and places it on a mound. Players may build onto new mounds or those of others. Cursed stones (with black marks) make the player lose their turn. Cursed stones are put aside after they are picked up. Placing 5 stones on a mound completes the grave. The player then has the option to unearth the mound or leave it.

UNEARTHING A GRAVE MOUND. Players unearth a grave by taking its Remains card:
- **Blank:** The dead does not return. Player is not affected.
- **Hand:** The dead has risen to kill another player out of the game. If the same player unearths **2** hands, they decide who gets killed. (Each hand can only be used once.)
- **White Skull:** The dead has risen, tried to attack and failed. If a player digs up 2 white skulls over the course of the game, they die.
- **Black Skull:** The site is cursed by an evil force. The dead has risen and killed the player.
- **Bone:** The dead has risen and wandered off aimlessly. Once 2 bones have been dug up, cursed stones **kill** those who pick them up.

Once all the mounds have been completed with 5 stones, players **must** unearth a mound each turn. Once unearthed, players keep Remains cards in front of them.

WINNING THE GAME. The game ends when only one player is left alive.

13
RUN FOR YOUR LIFE!

Circus Survival Game
based on Stephen King's *It!* (1990),
4–10 players

Some people have a real fear of clowns, and they just may have Stephen King to blame for it. If you or your friends have what has come to be known as coulrophobia, then watching Stephen King's *It!* is a great way to both scare and scar you for life.

The film was originally made for television and is split into two parts, the first focusing on the main characters in their childhood and the second in adulthood. As the ultimate symbol of terror, Pennywise the clown can get into the heads of his victims to resemble everything they were ever afraid of. And with each monstrous transformation, you may ask yourself which fate would be worse: facing such terror in the youthful days of innocence, or years later when you thought the nightmare was finally over.

THE GAME

In *Run for your Life!*, players watch Stephen King's *It!* to step into the roles of the characters on the screen, running from Pennywise and the many monsters he conveys. The TV room is turned into an old-fashioned circus to deeper resemble the world of the demented clown. With each scene, players must constantly be on the look out for the right cue to run for their lives if they hope to survive to the final credits. You will need:

Circus Items: • 27+ Balloons • 8 Pieces of Colored Construction Paper
• 4 Large Candy Bars • 4 Stuffed Animals • 2 Bags of Peanuts
• 3 Bags of Cotton Candy • Clown Wig • Clown Nose • Clown Horn
• Pair of Clown Shoes • 2 Different Colored Poster Boards
• 1–2 Rolls of String • Black Sharpie
Prizes: • Additional Circus Supplies or Candy Bags
Additional Supplies: • Scissors • Tape

PREPARING THE GAME

To make *Run for your Life!*, you'll need to prepare the following:
• Circus Décor • Balloons • Tags • Game Posters

CIRCUS DÉCOR. To set up your circus décor, arrange all your circus items throughout the TV room, putting the candy, stuffed animals, etc. on tables, shelves, windowsills and other easy-to-reach areas. Photocopy the Circus Posters and Circus Tickets below and tape each to a different wall. Balloons are a separate part of the circus décor and discussed below.

BALLOONS. Blow up 27 helium balloons as well as any additional balloons you choose to use for decoration. Use a black sharpie to write "Turn Back Now" on one balloon and tie it to the outside railing or porch for the first thing players see when they arrive. The remaining 26 balloons require tags and will be tied to various places around the TV room.

TAGS. Make 26 tags out of colored construction paper for the first half of the game, using big lettering so they can be seen from a distance. Make 2 of each tag:

1: Clothes Line	6: Shower Drain	11: Henry Bowers
2: Storm Drain	7: School Werewolf	12: Dead Lights
3: Ben's Dad	8: Lamppost	13: Grabbing Stan
4: Swamp Monster	9: Sewer Vents	
5: Sink Balloon	10: Sewer Pipe	

Tie each tag to a balloon and tape the balloons to tables, bookshelves, closet door handles, standing lamps and even the walls and floor in the TV room. Any extra balloons used for decoration should not have tags.

For the second part of the game, make an additional 22 tags out of construction paper. Write the following on these tags, then fold each **in half:**

Balloon (8 tags)	Silver Earring (2 tags)
Bike (6 tags)	Silver-Eyed Clown (2 tags)
Inhaler (3 tags)	Razor (1 tag)

Place these tags beside the circus items (candy, stuffed animals, etc.) around the TV room.

GAME POSTERS. Finally, make posters that list when players will be running for their lives throughout the game. You'll need one poster for each half of the movie. Refer to the samples below to make both posters out of red, blue or yellow poster board, using a different color for each. Use big lettering so that everyone in the room can read them from where they sit and hang them on either side of the TV.

PLAYING THE GAME

Before starting the movie, point out the game posters to the players. Each poster states specific scenes and times in the film that Pennywise appears or attacks, which is when everyone will need to run for their life.

FIRST HALF OF GAME AND FILM. Each time a scene is shown that is listed on the poster, **all** the players should be ready to run for a balloon. However, they must wait until the clown (or other monster Pennywise portrays) shows itself before running for it. At the correct time, players will only be searching for the balloons with the tags that match the specific scene. (Remember there are 2 of each.) Once the balloons are found, the players keep the tags but leave the balloons in place. The game continues in this fashion for the first half of the movie. When the first half is over, players count their tags.

SECOND HALF OF GAME AND FILM. For the second half of the movie, players will take the folded tags by the circus items but will take turns in choosing them rather than running at top speed. The two with the most tags from the first half of the film choose **1 tag** at the first Pennywise sighting, again waiting until the clown or creature appears in the scene listed on the poster. With each consecutive time Pennywise shows up, the next two players with the most tags take a folded tag. (If there is a tie, players decide amongst themselves.)

Folded tags do the following:
- **Balloon:** Player has been attacked by the clown. 2 attacks mean death!

- **Razor:** Player has killed him- or herself and is out of the game.
- **Silver Earring:** Takes away an attack from the clown on a future turn. (Cannot be used against attacks that have already been made.)
- **Inhaler:** Same effect as Silver Earring.
- **Bike:** Same effect as Silver Earring.
- **Silver-Eyed Clown:** Player has been paralyzed by the clown. The player is out of the game **unless** they are given the Bike tag by another player. If whoever had the Bike tag has already been killed, the player dies!

The player with the most tags from the first half of the game also has the option to **switch** their first tag with a different game item before choosing their second unless their first tag was a **Razor**. Players may give their Silver Earrings, Inhaler or Bike tags to players who have already been attacked by the clown to save their life on a future turn. However, they are not required to do this. The game ends when the movie is over. Anyone who survives wins a prize.

MAKE THIS GAME YOUR OWN!

Add to the circus atmosphere of Run for your Life! *with some old-fashioned popcorn boxes from your local party store for having popcorn during the film. Just keep in mind that when running for your life, the popcorn may* **fly***!*

You can also make your circus a bit more deadly by drizzling fake blood on your front steps and on any balloons you place outside, as well as using scarred and demented stuffed animals from your Dolls from Hell *game in Chapter 11.*

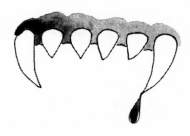

Run for your Life!

Object of the Game

Run from Pennywise to make it to the end of the film alive.

FIRST HALF OF THE MOVIE AND GAME. Each time Pennywise appears or attacks in the scene listed on the game poster, **all players** run for the balloons to find the tags listing the current scene. Players take the tags but leave the balloons in place.

After the first half of the film, players count their tags.

SECOND HALF OF THE MOVIE AND GAME. Two players each choose a tag from a circus item when Pennywise attacks in the scene listed on the poster. The players with the most tags from the first half of the film choose during the first Pennywise attack, those with the second most tags choose on the second attack, and so on.

CIRCUS ITEM TAGS

- **Balloon:** Player has been attacked by the clown. 2 attacks mean death!
- **Razor:** Player has killed him- or herself and is out of the game.
- **Silver Earring:** Takes away an attack from Pennywise on a future turn. (Cannot be used against attacks that have already been made.)
- **Inhaler:** Same effect as Silver Earring.
- **Bike:** Same effect as Silver Earring.
- **Silver-Eyed Clown:** Player has been paralyzed by the clown. They are out of the game unless they are given the **Bike tag** by another player. If the one with the Bike tag has already been killed, they die, too!

The player with the most tags from the first half of the game has the option to switch their first tag with different game item before choosing their second unless their first tag was a **Razor**.

WINNING THE GAME. The game ends when the movie is over. Anyone who has made it out alive wins a prize.

Game Posters

Part 1

Clothes Line — 4 min

Storm Drain — 11 min

Ben's Dad — 30 min

Swamp Monster — 30 min

Sink Balloon — 42 min

Shower Drain — 51 min

School Werewolf — 59 min

Lamppost — 1 hr, 9 min

Sewer Vents — 1 hr, 22 min

Sewer Pipe — 1 hr, 24 min

Henry Bowers — 1 hr, 25 min

Dead Lights — 1 hr, 26 min

Grabbing Stan — 1 hr, 29 min

Part 2

Grave — 98 sec

Library Clown — 6 min

Swamp Skeleton — 12 min

Pharmacist — 16 min

Old Lady — 19 min

Mummy — 39 min

Fridge Head — 41 min

Mental Hospital — 46 min

Gas Station — 52 min

Kissing Clown — 69 min

Huge Spider — 1 hr, 22 min

COPY @ 120%

Circus Posters

Circus Tickets

14
HELL AND DAMNATION

Vampire Journal Game
based on *Interview with the Vampire (1994)*,
3–6 players

In *Interview with the Vampire*, you won't see the castle-dwelling, bat-like vampires of yesteryear. These creatures of the night are human-looking and intelligent, suave and sophisticated. They are seen from their mortal days, young and struggling with the pains of life until ultimately becoming one of the immortal — and damned.

Several types of vampires are presented in the film reflecting various vampire cultural legends. But not all are beautiful, and not all desire company. What these monsters *do* share is the struggle of enduring eternity to explore the night, prey on the living and keep an eye out for their own kind.

THE GAME

In this vampire journal game, players take on the roles of specific types of vampires from both Anne Rice's *Vampire Chronicles* and various vampire myths. Each player keeps a journal of their nightly activities while trying to keep their identities secret so as not to get discovered and killed. Journals resemble the Hell and Damnation book from the film and contain actual beliefs on vampires and vampire lore from around the world. You will need:

- 19 Gold Coins • 7 Black Stones • 2 Sheets Black Cardstock • Red Paint
- Fine Paint Brush • Scissors • Double-Sided Tape • Stapler

PREPARING THE GAME

To make *Hell and Damnation*, you'll need to prepare the following:
- Vampire Journals • Death Stones • Game Cards
- Game Card Meaning Sheets

VAMPIRE JOURNALS. Photocopy the pages below to make one Vampire Journal for each player. Use a double-sided copier to staple the pages in the following order:

Hell and Damnation Cover Page

Game Introduction and Rules

5 Character Pages *(placed in **different orders** in each journal)*

Doomed to Become Vampires

Journal Page

Vampire: Egyptian Vampire

Journal Page

Protecting the Living

Journal Page

Vampire: Old World Vampire

Journal Page

Protecting the Dead

Journal Page

Vampire: Animal Vampire

Journal Page

Signs of a Vampire

Journal Page

Vampire: 18th Century Vampire

Journal Page

Seductions of a Vampire

Journal Page

Vampire: Modern Vampire

Journal Page

Notes Pages (2)

DEATH STONES. To make the Death Stones, purchase 7 black stones from your local craft store and write one of the following on each with red paint:

Sun	Bullet	Decapitate
Stake	Holy Water	
Fire	Bible	

GAME CARDS can be made by photocopying the images below and taping them onto 3.5 × 3.5" pieces of black cardstock. Make 2 of each for a total of 14 cards.

GAME CARD MEANING SHEETS. Finally, photocopy the Game Cards Meaning sheet so there is one for each player.

PLAYING THE GAME

Each player is given a vampire journal, pen, Game Card Meanings sheet, 3 coins and 1 Death Stone chosen at random. Remaining Death Stones and 1 coin are put in the middle of the table. Game cards are shuffled and placed face down on the table.

Throughout the game, players will make journal entries of their nightly activities as a vampire based on 1 Game card they are dealt. Players will want to accumulate points, coins, and try to figure out which player is which type of vampire.

The order of play is as follows each turn:

Deal Cards
Write in Journal
Take Death Stones or Coins
Read another's Journal Entry
Kill other Vampires

JOURNAL ENTRIES. Players begin by turning to the first topic page in their journal (*Doomed to become a Vampire*) and getting dealt 2 cards. They choose 1 of the 2 cards they are dealt and keep it face up. They then draw the symbol of the card (or simply write the name of it) on their Journal Page and write a short sentence about what they did that night that relates its topic, referring to the Game Card Meaning Sheet and the Character page of their journal for tips on what to write. Any bit of information can be written that relates to that card, such as:

- *Skull:* Info on when they became a vampire: year, place, age, by force or choice
- *Hourglass:* Their physical appearance or current age
- *Moon:* Things they do during the night when not feeding
- *Fangs:* Different kinds of vampires they've come into contact with based on where they are
- *Blood:* Types of people they kill, based on where they go & what they do
- *Coffin:* A time they went into deep rest or woke up again, how long they rested for or how long since they've had a long rest
- *Grave:* Where they keep quarters and sleep during the day, how old they are

An example of what an Egyptian Vampire may write for different cards may include:
- Coffin: *Rose in 1850*
- Blood: *Fed off Ship Captain*

- Grave: *Sleep under the sand*
- Hourglass: *I have dark skin*
- Fangs: *Met a Modern Vampire*

Players get 1 point if the card they use is the same symbol shown on their current journal page.

EXTRA PLAYS. After the journal entries have been written, players then take any extra plays their card allows. Players can only take extra plays for the card they chose for their journal entry.

- *Fangs:* Player can read someone's journal entry to "read their thoughts." (However, the other player may pay 2 coins to the table to prevent someone from looking at their journal.) Players get 1 point if they go through the topic page of their own kind of vampire with no one reading their journal.
- *Skull:* Player can take a Death Stone from the table. If there are no more Death Stones on the table, the player can take a stone from another player if they pay them 1 coin. (*If 2 players use this card and the first one takes the last Death Stone in the center of the table, the next player can then take one from a player for 1 coin.*)
- *2 Skulls:* If a player is dealt 2 Skulls on the same hand, they may take a Death Stone from another player instead of the table. 2 Skulls also means the player can no longer get points on that page unless they pay 1 coin to the center that turn.
- *Hourglass:* Once the **third** set of cards has been dealt for that journal page, the player who uses the Hourglass decides if they stay on that page or move on to the next. **Each page is played for no less than 3 turns and no more than 5 turns.** If no one uses the Hourglass on the third turn, the game continues to the forth turn and then the fifth.
- *Moon:* Player can take all the coins from the table. If 2 players use the Moon card, the coins are split evenly, keeping one on the table for an odd number. If there is only 1 coin, the player closest to the left of the dealer takes it. Any coins put on the table this turn cannot be taken.
- *Blood:* Gives 1 point.
- *Coffin:* No extra play.
- *2 Coffins:* If a player is dealt 2 Coffins on the same hand, they go into deep rest and take no action this turn. The player cannot pay to keep someone from reading their journal.
- *Grave:* No extra play.

Extra plays are played starting with the person **to the left of the dealer and** moving clockwise. **A new player deals with each new page.**

KILLING VAMPIRES. Players will want to accumulate Death Stones throughout the game to kill off players once they discover what kind of vampire they are. This information is found by reading each other's journals. Each type of vampire requires 3 Death Stones to kill them. Players must have a total of 3 Death Stones before they can give them to another player to try and kill them. Once this is done, if a player has been dealt stones that do not kill them, they take **1 stone** that has no effect and it goes back to the table. The player who attempted to kill them loses 1 point and takes back the remaining stones. The only thing that kills a player is getting all 3 of their Death Stones at once. If a vampire is successfully killed, the player who killed him earns **5 points.**

When a player is killed, they can still play the game, but cannot win. They are still dealt cards each turn and write in their journal, but they cannot take coins, Death Stones or decide whether or not to move to the next page.

PASSING TIME. Each new journal page represents a different year. Whenever possible, players should try to **relate** all the information on each page, as if they are writing about a certain location and events that happened there. *(For example, if a player uses a Blood card first turn, they may write that they fed on a rich millionaire in the city. If they then use a Moon card, they may say that they visited an art museum in the city. If they then use Fangs, they may say they came into contact with Modern Vampires.)*

Players should change information with each new page so that they travel, sleep and rise in different times. Players should avoid using the same information twice in the game.

WINNING THE GAME. The game continues until the last page is reached. The player who uses the Hourglass once again decides to stop after 3 turns (if they have enough points to win, they should!) or continue. Points are then added up, and the surviving vampire with the most points wins:

- *1 point:* Each played Game card matching the symbol on the current journal page.
- *1 point:* No one reads a player's journal when the topic page is their type of vampire.
- *1 point:* Using the Fangs card.
- *5 points:* Killing a vampire.
- *5 points:* Most coins at the end of the game. If there is a tie, players get 1 point each.

Tips:

- You may choose to move to the **next** journal page if you have written something in your journal that you don't want another play to see. You may also want to stop before other players have the option of gaining additional points if you are currently in the lead.
- You may want to **stay** on a current journal page to get more points yourself or to have the opportunity to read journals since multiple cards have been played on that page so there will be more written information.
- Players can try to fool others with journal entries that can be misleading. For example: an 18th century vampire may travel to Egypt, and thereby is correct in writing that he or she slept in the sand. This may look like they are an Egyptian vampire if someone reads their journal. Likewise, an Egyptian vampire may write "Paris" to signify visiting there during a Moon cast. This could be misinterpreted as being an 18th century vampire.

MAKE THIS GAME YOUR OWN!

You can also make your vampire journals out of blank journals or small notebooks, cutting and taping the pages into the books rather than stapling them together.

Hell and Damnation

Object of the Game

Accumulate points through your undead doings
while trying to keep your identity hidden.

Players begin with a vampire journal, Game Card Sheet, 3 coins and Death Stone chosen at random. Remaining Death Stones and 1 coin are put in the middle of the table along with the game cards kept face down. Each turn, players turn to the same page of their journal and are dealt 2 cards. Journal pages are used in order.

ORDER OF PLAY. Deal Cards * Write in Journal * Take Death Stones or Coins * Read Journals * Kill Players

JOURNAL ENTRIES. Players choose 1 of their cards and turn it face up. They draw or write the card's symbol on their journal page along with a short sentence relating to its topic. Players refer to their Game Card Sheets and Character Pages of their journal for examples on what to write, and should avoid using the same information twice. Using the card that matches the symbol on the current journal page earns 1 point. Each new Journal Page represents a new year in which players should alter their entries, including where they were and what they did. After writing journal entries, players make any extra plays their card allows, starting with the player to the left of the dealer and moving clockwise.

JOURNAL PAGES are used for a minimum of 3 plays and a maximum of 5. In the third play, the player who uses the Hourglass decides if they stay on the current page or continue to the next. If no Hourglasses are played, the game continues on the current page until the fifth turn. If 2 players use the Hourglass, the decision of moving to the next page trumps staying on the current page. A new player deals the cards with each new journal page.

KILLING VAMPIRES. Players can use the Fangs card to look at each others' journals and figure out what type of vampires they are. They can then try to kill them by giving them 3 Death Stones. Killing a vampire earns **5 points**. If 1 or more stones have effect but they are not the correct 3, the player admits 1 of the stones that can be used to kill them. 1 stone without effect is put back to the table and the remaining 2 are returned to the player who **loses 1 point**.

WINNING THE GAME. The game ends when all the pages have been played and the surviving player with the most points wins:

- *1 point:* Each played Game card matching the symbol on the current journal page.
- *1 point:* No one reads a player's journal when the topic page is their type of vampire.
- *1 point:* Using the Fangs card.
- *5 points:* Killing a vampire.
- *5 points:* Most coins at the end of the game. If there is a tie, players each get 1 point.

Game Card Meanings Sheet

Journal Entries & Extra Plays

 ### WHEN YOU BECAME A VAMPIRE
Take a Death Stone from the table. If there are no more Death Stones, take a stone from another player if you pay them 1 coin.

 ### TWO SKULLS ON THE SAME HAND
Take a Death Stone from another player instead of the table. You can no longer get points on this page unless you pay 1 coin to the table.

 ### YOUR PHYSICAL APPEARANCE OR AGE
On or after the 3rd play, choose to either stay on the current journal page next turn or continue to the next page.

 ### PLACES YOU GO/THINGS YOU DO WHEN NOT FEEDING
Take all the coins from the table. (If 2 players use the Moon card, coins are split. If there is only 1 coin, the player closest to the left of the dealer takes it. Cannot take any coins added to the table this turn.)

 ### VAMPIRES YOU'VE COME INTO CONTACT WITH
Choose a player to read their mind (current page of their journal). *Other player can pay 2 coins to the table to prevent this.*

 ### TYPES OF PEOPLE YOU KILL
Gives 1 point.

 ### TIMES OF LONG REST WHEN TAKEN, ARISEN, HOW LONG YOU SLEPT

  ### TWO COFFINS ON THE SAME HAND
You go into deep rest. No actions taken and no points gained. You cannot pay to keep someone from reading your journal.

 ### WHERE YOU SLEEP OR RETREAT TO/CURRENT AGE
No extra play.

ORDER OF PLAY
Deal Cards * Write in Journal * Take Death Stones or Coins
* Read Journals *Kill Players

HELL
AND
DAMNATION

VAMPIRE LEGENDS have abounded throughout the centuries. They vary with country and culture, each containing different methods for preventing their development, keeping them away and ultimately destroying them.

One aspect prevalent in all legends is that vampires are secretive, even with each other, and giving themselves away could mean their own destruction...

THE GAME

Choose your vampire type.
Use 1 of your 2 Game Cards per turn, writing something
based on the card in your journal.
Make any additional plays your card allows.

THROUGHOUT THE GAME

Try to figure out which player is what kind of vampire by reading their journals.
Once you know, kill them by giving them 3 Death Stones.

WINNING THE GAME

Points are accrued through symbols, coins and killing off other vampires. At the
end of the game, the player with the most points wins.

Egyptian Vampire

Killed By: Decapitation, Stake, Bible

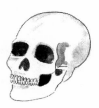

SKULL You became a vampire roughly 2,500 B.C.E. You were 26 and the slave of a Pharaoh who turned you by force.

HOURGLASS You're 4,500 years old. You have dark skin, fine facial features, dark eyes and black hair.

MOON You often visit places and people of great power: big cities, temples, Kings, Monarchs, Presidents.

BLOOD You feed on poachers and tomb robbers of Egypt and tourists while traveling. You always feed during the full moon and often fast in between.

COFFIN Since 1,000 A.D. you've gone into long rests for up to 300 years when times get dull.

FANGS You've encountered other Egyptian vampires and 18th century vampires traveling the country.

GRAVE You sleep in the deserts in Egypt and below the dirt when traveling.

Old World Vampire

Killed By: Sun, Stake, Fire

SKULL

You became a vampire in the 16th century in Eastern Europe. You were killed by an Old World vampire at 32 and rose from the dead the next night, and every night thereafter.

HOURGLASS

You have red, puffy skin and rotting flesh. You wear the cloths you were buried in: a white shroud now torn to rags. You smell of decay and rot.

MOON

You like to prowl through the dark and dirty streets of small towns and graveyards.

BLOOD

You kill anyone who is out after dark, but are unable to break into homes.

COFFIN

Every few hundred years you go into long rests for an average of 50 years.

FANGS

You've encountered 18th century vampires and other Old World vampires throughout your undead lifetime.

GRAVE

You sleep in crypts in old cemeteries and ruins.

Modern Vampire

Killed By: Fire, Bullet, Holy Water

SKULL You became a vampire in the 1980s. You were 19 and living in Chicago. You were made by another Modern vampire, and didn't know what you were doing when he turned you.

HOURGLASS You're 45 but still look 19. You have pale skin with short, black hair and always dress in black.

MOON You spend your time in Chicago in rock clubs, movie theaters, parties of mortals and immortals alike.

BLOOD You kill clueless rock and punk kids, cops who bust into night clubs and anyone who gives you the wrong look.

COFFIN You sleep daily, and have yet to go into any kind of long rest.

FANGS You've come across other Modern vampires and some 18th century vampires who drift by.

GRAVE You sleep in a coffin in the basement of abandoned homes.

18th Century Vampire

Killed By: Sun, Fire, Decapitation

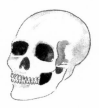

SKULL	You became a vampire at 21 during the 18th century in Russia. You were encountered by an Egyptian vampire who persuaded you to become immortal.
HOURGLASS	You're almost 300 years old. You are tall, thin, have long hair and pale skin.
MOON	You like to visit cities throughout the world and view the arts, including theaters, galleries, museums and the like.
BLOOD	You tend to feed off the rich and their servants.
COFFIN	When you take long rests, you sleep for no more than 25–50 years so that you don't miss much.
FANGS	You've encountered Modern vampires in clubs and theaters, making fools of themselves.
GRAVE	You sleep in an expensive coffin in the homes of rich families you kill.

COPY @ 120%

Animal Vampire

Killed By: Bullet, Holy Water, Bible

SKULL   You became a vampire in 1485 at the age of 36. You were living in Serbia and killed by an animal vampire. You rose from the dead the next night.

HOURGLASS   You have long, pointy ears, long thin fingers and a small nose. You can take on the shape of a bat, wolf or rat at will, as well as turn into mist to get under doors and windows.

MOON   When not feeding, you roam the forests, mountains and valleys.

BLOOD   You generally feed off those wandering in the woods or who live close to the woods. You also feed off small animals.

COFFIN   Every thousand years or so you take long rests for up to 200 years at a time.

FANGS   You've encountered very few Animal vampires, but many Old World vampires within the forests.

GRAVE   You sleep under dirt and mud in the woods.

Doomed to Become Vampires

In old myths, being bitten by a vampire was not the only way a person was believed to become one...

A person could become a vampire if they had led a particularly evil life. Also, if they were born with a caul, tail, or born out of wedlock, died an unnatural death, committed suicide or died before baptism.

Other beliefs included being the 7th child of the same sex in a family or the child of a woman who didn't eat salt.

Egyptian Vampire

Egyptian vampires always feed during the full moon and may fast in between.
They may rest for up to 300 years at a time.
Killed By: Decapitation, Stake, Bible

Throughout the centuries, almost every culture in the world has had legends of the undead consuming the flesh and blood of the living. In ancient times, the concept of a vampire did not exist, and these activities were believed to be the work of demons and spirits.

Protecting the Living

The following was used throughout Europe to protect the living against vampires:

Garlic	Crucifix
Holy Water	Rosary Beads
Wild Rose	Consecrated Ground
Hawthorn Plant	Running Water
Mustard Seeds	Mirrors

Some traditions also held that a vampire cannot enter a home unless invited. If a vampire was believed to be at work, the body of the one accused was exhumed. Their head was severed and their heart or even entire body was burned.

Old World Vampire

Old World vampires are not conscious beings but merely animated corpses. They have bloated skin, stink of death and sleep in crypts and ruins.
Killed By: Sun, Stake, Fire

The ignorance of widespread disease attributed much to belief in vampires in the 18th and 19th centuries. The bubonic plague and tuberculosis were highly contagious and often extinguished entire families. Each involved the breakdown of lung tissue which caused blood to appear on the lips after death.

Protecting the Dead

Methods to protect the dead from becoming vampires included crossing the arms of the corpse, placing a cross or crucifix on the grave or burying the person at the junction of a crossroads. With the start of Christianity, religious authorities stated that if families did not bury their loved ones by the rites of the church, which included paying a fee to their priest, the deceased would return from the dead to kill them for their neglect.

Animal Vampire

Animal vampires resemble animals and possess the ability to shape shift into them. They live in forests and only come into civilization to feed.
Killed By: Bullet, Holy Water, Bible

It was not until Bram Stoker's publication of *Dracula* in 1897 that vampire legends involved taking on the form of animals and mist to more easily acquire their prey.

COPY @ 120%

Signs of a Vampire

Signs that a vampire is in the area include:
- Death of cattle, sheep, relatives or neighbors of one who has recently died
- Exhumed bodies found in a lifelike state with apparent new growth of fingernails or hair
- Exhumed bodies swelled with a reddish complexion or blood on the mouth

In some reports, vampires were said to possess phantom-like attributes, assuming the form of a dark mass or being completely transparent. Rather than being a physical entity, the creature was a spirit connected to the corpse it once animated. This reaffirmed the belief that a vampire could rise from its coffin to feed without disturbing the soil of its grave.

18th Century Vampire

18th century vampires were born to darkness during the Enlightenment,
and often take a liking to the arts and theater.
They travel often and carefully choose their victims.
Killed By: Sun, Fire, Decapitation

In the 18th century, a large number of vampire sightings were reported in Eastern Europe, resulting in a vampire mass hysteria throughout the continent. Thousands of corpses were exhumed and staked, and living people were even accused of vampirism.

Seductions of a Vampire

In ancient legends, vampires resembled living corpses and took no pleasure from their victims, who served merely as food. Over the centuries as Christianity evolved, tales adapted into vampires taking on the form of living human beings, and drinking blood became a sensual desire for both the vampire and its victim.

Modern Vampire

Modern vampires have only been around since the mid–20th century.
They often dress in black and can easily blend in with mortals.
Killed By: Fire, Bullet, Holy Water

In modern tales, a vampire is killed by driving a stake through its heart. However, staking vampires in the past consisted of pinning the corpse to the ground, thus preventing it from rising from its grave.

COPY @ 120%

Notes

COPY @ 120%

Notes

Total Points

Journal Page

Points

Journal Page

Points

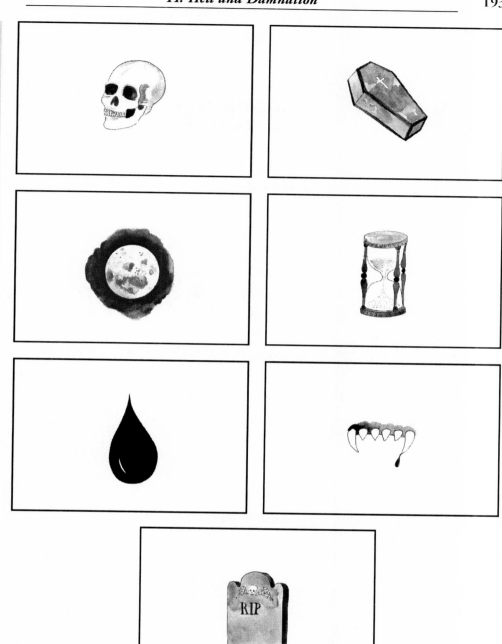

15
SURROUNDED

Zombie Card Game
based on *Resident Evil (2002)*,
3–5 players

Resident Evil is one of the best modern zombie movies. Based on the video game from the late 1990s, the seemingly everyday office atmosphere of the Umbrella Corporation suddenly turns deadly in a matter of seconds, sending a shiver down our spine each time the fire drill goes off at work.

The film also provides a great background story for the creation of the T virus. There is no residue from other planets or toxic radiation responsible for turning people into the living dead here, but rather carefully tested chemicals engineered by our own scientists and supercomputers. And since supercomputers aren't affected by the outbreak like their human creators, they are the ones that will decide how to keep the virus contained ... no matter what the cost.

THE GAME

In this zombie card game, players take on the roles of either marines or zombies down in the Hive. The marines have been sent in to shut down the Red Queen for trapping and destroying everyone in the building after the virus was released. Zombies, on the other hand, will try to turn all the marines into their own kind before they can reach their target. You will need:
- 77 3 × 5" Plain Index Cards   • Scissors   • Double-Sided Tape

PREPARING THE GAME

To make *Surrounded*, you'll need to put together 2 types of cards:
- Character Cards   • Playing Cards

CHARACTER CARDS. To make the Character cards, photocopy the images below and attach each to a 2¼ × 2¾" plain index card with double-sided tape. (These are easily made by cutting off ⅓ of 3 × 5" plain index cards.) You'll need 4 Humans and 1 Zombie Character card in all.

PLAYING CARDS can also photocopied below and taped onto 2¼ × 2¾" plain index cards. Some of the Playing card images require multiple copies to make the following 72 cards:
- 30 Zombies   • 10 Action cards   • 6 Guns   • 6 Blades   • 6 *10 Minutes Pass* cards
- 5 Bombs   • 3 *Red Queen Shut Down* 1 cards   • 2 *Red Queen Shut Down* 2 cards
- 2 Antivirus cards   • 1 *Red Queen Shut Down* 3 card   • 1 Monster

PLAYING THE GAME

To start the game, each player is given a Character card that is kept face up in front of them. The number of players determines how many Humans and Zombies start the game:
- *2–3 players:* All begin as Humans.
- *4–5 players:* 1 player begins as a Zombie, the rest as Humans.

Each player is then dealt 2 Playing cards. The goal for the Humans is to shut down the Red Queen within 1 hour. The goal for the Zombies is to turn all other players into Zombies. With each turn, players pick up cards so that they have 3. (This does not include their Character card.) They play anywhere from **1** to **all of their cards** each turn, putting them in a face up discard pile. Players may discard as many cards at the end of their turn as they wish, and may keep up to 2 cards at the end of their turn before discarding to the discard pile. Throughout the game, Humans will want to play Red Queen Shut Down cards, Human Advantage cards and kill off as many zombie cards as they can. Zombies will want to assign zombie cards to Humans and play Zombie Advantage cards.

ZOMBIES. Any zombie cards that Humans pick up are immediately put down in front of them. *If a player has been dealt zombie cards at the start of the game, they immediately put them into play and pick up additional cards on their first turn so they have 3.* Zombie cards remain in front of the player until they are killed off with weapons. Any zombie cards that Zombies pick up are immediately put down in front a **Human**. Zombies may choose which Human to assign their zombie cards to each turn.

BECOMING A ZOMBIE. When a Human has **5 or more** zombies in front of them, they turn into a Zombie. (The Monster counts as 3 zombies.) The player begins to take actions of a Zombie to turn all other players into Zombies on their **next** turn. As soon as a player becomes a Zombie, they put down any cards in their hand that are not Zombie Action cards for Humans to pick up. These cards remain face up in front of them. (Picking up a card from a Zombie counts as taking a card from the draw pile.) On the Zombie's next turn, any of their cards that were not picked up by Humans are put in the discard pile, and the player continues to hold up to 3 cards in their hand from this point on.

If at any time a player **begins** their turn with 5 zombies (Ex: a Zombie player has given them a few zombies since their last turn), they will become a Zombie **only** if they cannot kill the required amount of zombies before the **end** of their turn.

ACTION CARDS can either be played immediately or saved. There are 5 action cards that help Humans, and 5 that help Zombies.

The **ANTIVIRUS** can either protect a player from turning into a Zombie **or** turn a player back into a Human if they are already a Zombie. If they are Human, they can use the antivirus to get rid of up to 5 zombie cards in front of them. If they have less than 5 zombies, the antivirus is put on their current zombie cards, and the next zombies they get are applied to it. Zombie cards and the antivirus are then put into the discard pile. If the player is already a Zombie, the antivirus automatically turns them Human again. However, getting 5 zombie cards from this point on will turn them back into a Zombie. Players can assign the antivirus to themselves or to another player.

WEAPONS. There are 3 kinds of weapons in the game: guns and blades which kill 1 zombie at a time and bombs that kill up to 3 zombies **or** the Monster. Weapons can be used to kill a player's own zombies or those of another player, but can only be used on the player's turn.

SHUTTING DOWN THE RED QUEEN. Humans must shut down the Red Queen to win the game. This is done by putting down 3 Break In cards in the correct order (1, 2 and 3) to the right of the draw pile. Although there are more than one Break In 1 and 2 cards, each only needs to be put down **once**.

RACING THE CLOCK. 10 Minutes Pass cards make time go by. When picked up, they are immediately put down above the draw pile. The game ends in 1 hour when the sixth *10 Minutes Pass* card has been put down, as the Red Queen has shut everyone in the Hive for good.

WINNING THE GAME. The game ends when either:
- The Humans shut down the Red Queen and win,
- All players are turned into Zombies, and the Zombies win, or
- The sixth *10 Minutes Pass* card is played and no one wins!

Tips:

- As a Human, protect your teammates as much as yourself from turning into a Zombie ... if not, they'll be coming after you next!
- Don't be too quick to discard cards that are beneficial to Zombies. If you get turned into a Zombie later on, that card may help you win!

LIKE THIS GAME?

Check out You're Next! *in Chapter 2 for another card game of survival of the species!*

Surrounded

Object of the Game

Humans: Shut down the Red Queen in 1 hour.
Zombies: Turn all players into Zombies.
2–3 Players: All players start as Humans.
4–5 Players: 1 player starts as a Zombie, the rest Human.

All players begin with a Character card and 2 Playing cards. Character cards are kept face up in front of the players, and remaining Playing cards are kept face down as the draw pile. With each turn, a player draws so that they have 3 cards and plays anywhere from **1** to **all** of their cards. Played cards are put in a face up discard pile. Players may discard as many cards as they wish at the end of their turn, but may keep a max of 2 cards in their hand. Throughout the game Humans will want to play Red Queen Shut Down cards, Human Advantage cards and kill off as many zombie cards as they can. Zombies will want to assign zombie cards to Humans and play Zombie Advantage cards.

Any **ZOMBIE CARDS** that Humans pick up are immediately put down in front of them. Any zombie cards that Zombies pick up are immediately put down in front of a **Human**. *Any zombie cards dealt at the start of the game are immediately put into play and players pick up extra cards on their first turn for a total of 3 cards.*

BECOMING A ZOMBIE. When a Human has 5 or more zombies in front of them at the **end** of their turn, they turn into a Zombie. (The Monster counts as 3 zombies.) They immediately put down any cards in their hand that are not Zombie Action cards for Humans to pick up. (Picking up a card from a Zombie counts as taking a card from the draw pile.) These cards are discarded on the Zombie's next turn, and the player continues to hold up to 3 cards from this point on. If at any time a player begins their turn with 5 zombies (Ex: a Zombie player has given them a few zombies since their last turn), they will become a Zombie only if they cannot kill the required amount of zombies before the **end** of their turn. When players become Zombies, they take on the roles of Zombies on their next turn.

ACTION CARDS can either be played immediately or saved. Some action cards help Humans, while others help Zombies.

SHUTTING DOWN THE RED QUEEN. Humans shut down the Red Queen by putting down 3 Break In cards in the correct order (1, 2 and 3) to the right of the draw pile.

ANTIVIRUS. Using the antivirus on a Zombie turns the Zombie back into a Human. However, they can turn into a Zombie again if they get 5 zombie cards in front of them. Using the antivirus on a Human protects them from 5 zombie cards. If they have less than 5 zombies in front of them, it is put on their current zombie cards and the next zombies they get are applied to it. After use, the antivirus and zombies are put into the discard pile. A player can use the antivirus on themselves **or** another player.

WEAPONS can be used to kill a player's own zombies **or** the zombies of another player. A player can only use or give a weapon on their own turn. After use, weapons and zombies are put into the discard pile.

RACING THE CLOCK. When a 10 Minutes Pass card is picked up, it is immediately put down above the draw pile. Humans have only 1 hour to shut down the Red Queen to win, and Zombies have only 1 hour to turn all the Humans into Zombies to win.

WINNING THE GAME. The game ends when either:
• The Humans shut down the Red Queen and win,
• All players are turned into Zombies, and the Zombies win, or
• The sixth *10 Minutes Pass* card is played and no one wins.

Character Cards

Character Card:
HUMAN

Character Card:
HUMAN

Character Card:
HUMAN

Character Card:
HUMAN

Character Card:
ZOMBIE

COPY @ 120%

Playing Cards

Weapon
Gun

Single Use.

Weapon
Gun

Single Use.

Weapon
Gun

Single Use.

Weapon
Blade

Single Use.

Weapon
Blade

Single Use.

Weapon
Blade

Single Use.

Weapon
Bomb

Kills up to 3 Zombies.

Weapon
Bomb

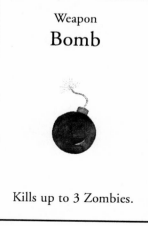

Kills up to 3 Zombies.

Weapon
Bomb

Kills up to 3 Zombies.

COPY @ 120%

Playing Cards

Zombie

Zombie

Zombie

Zombie

Zombie

Zombie

Zombie

Zombie

Zombie

COPY @ 120%

Action Cards

Action Card
Weak Zombies

Guns and Blades kill
2 Zombies instead
of 1 this turn.

Action Card
Hacker Trick

A human may search
through the draw pile and
take any Shutdown Card.
Play only after 30 min.
have passed.

Action Card
Zombie Drift

All Zombie players must
put down 1 card from
their hand for any
human to take.

Action Card
Human Advantage

A human may take
2 cards from the discard
pile this turn.

Action Card
Red Queen Trap

1 weapon in each player's
hand breaks and must
be discarded.

Action Card
Multiplying Zombies

Zombies move under cover
of darkness. Each zombie
card counts as 2 this turn.

Action Card
Red Queen Trap

Any antivirus a player is
holding breaks and must
be discarded.

Action Card
Monster Sneaks Up

Monster attacks 1
player this turn.
(Counts as 3 zombies)

Action Card
Zombie Advantage

A zombie can take 2
cards from the discard
pile this turn.

Action Card

Stupid Zombies

2 zombies per player get themselves killed from their own stupidity.

Antivirus

Removes 5 zombies or changes a Zombie player back to Human.

Monster

Does damage of 3 zombies.

Red Queen

Shut Down

1

Red Queen

Shut Down

2

Red Queen

Shut Down

3

10 Minutes Pass

10 Minutes Pass

10 Minutes Pass

COPY @ 120%

THE NEVERENDING NIGHTMARE

    You've survived. Perhaps barely. Or perhaps not at all, but you somehow managed to come back for more.

    Now that you've become an expert on the world of surviving demonic creatures and psycho killers, how has it changed the way you watch your favorite monster films? You and your battle-scarred friends have been attacked by a killer clown, turned into a human fly, dug up long lost relatives in the cemetery and banished evil spirits out of possessed dolls. Who was the conquering hero? Who revealed their true killer nature? And who knew right off the bat to hide a vial of poison up their sleeve? After each game and movie adventure, you may have started to feel that closer connection to the heroes and victims of the films — or more admiration for the villains who slaughtered them all.

As the creator of these games, you now have a monstrous collection complete with enough body parts, lab experiments and dance party CDs to keep the madness going. If you've already gone through each game in this book, don't worry: the fun isn't over. Flip back to your favorites and alter the scenarios and storylines, game cards and props so that the next round will be completely different and new adventures can unfold.

Of course, don't feel the need to limit yourself to the games and films in this book alone. Think about your other favorite monster flicks that aren't covered here. Think about chainsaw-wielding slayers, undead creatures of the night and other-worldly beings that have always held a place in your heart. These types of monsters can set the stage for modeling new game creations, or you can seek out titles you've never explored before for unleashing unknown nightmares into the world.

After all, what's life without a little shock, gore and hellfire? One just might fall into an eternal sleep without them, never to see the light of day again. To stay on the safe side, step into the world of parties and games to let your inner monster run free with horror, thrills and fun again and again.

BIBLIOGRAPHY

Achilli, Justin, Andrew Bates, Phil Brucato, Richard E. Danksy, Ed Hall, Robert Hatch, and Michael B. Lee. *Vampire: The Masquerade*. Stone Mountain, GA: White Wolf, 1998.

Carroll, Noel. *The Philosophy of Horror*. New York: Routledge, 1990.

Cavendish, Richard. *The Black Arts*. New York: Perigee Books, 1983.

Curran, Dr. Bob. *Vampires: A Field Guide to the Creatures that Stalk the Night*. Franklin Lakes, NJ: Career Press, 2005.

Greer, John Michael. *The New Encyclopedia of the Occult*. St. Paul, MN: Llewellyn, 2003.

Gregory, Constantine. *The Vampire Watcher's Handbook: A Guide for Slayers*. New York: St. Martin's Press, 2003.

Hardy, Phil. *The Overlook Film Encyclopedia: Horror*. New York: Overlook Press, 1994.

Hutchings, Peter. *The Horror Film*. Essex, England: Pierson Education, 2004.

Jones, Alan. *The Rough Guide to Horror Movies*. New York: Rough Guides, 2005.

Jones, Darryl. *Horror: A Thematic History in Fiction & Film*. New York: Oxford University Press, 2002.

Kachuba, John. *Ghosthunters: On the Trail of Mediums, Dowsers, Spirit Seekers, and Other Investigators of America's Paranormal World*. Franklin Lakes, NJ: Career Press, 2007.

Konstantinos. *Vampires: The Occult Truth*. St. Paul, MN: Llewellyn, 2003.

Marmell, Ari, Dean Shomshak, and C.A. Suleiman. *Vampire: The Requiem*. Stone Mountain, GA: White Wolf, 2004.

Meikle, Denis. *Vincent Price: The Art of Fear*. Richmond, Surrey (UK): Reynolds & Hearn, 2006.

Melton, Gordon J. *The Vampire Book: The Encyclopedia of the Undead*. Visible Ink Press, 1998.

Rice, Anne. *Interview with the Vampire*. New York: Random House, 1976.

_____. *Queen of the Damned*. New York: Ballantine, 1988.

_____. *The Vampire Lestat*. New York: Ballantine, 1985.

Skal, David J. *The Monster Show: The Cultural History of Horror*. New York: Faber and Faber, 1993.

_____. *Vampires: Encounters with the Undead*. New York: Black Dog and Leventhal, 2001.

Sledzik, Paul S. and Nicholas Bellantoni. "Bioarcheological and Biocultural Evidence for the New England Vampire Folk Belief." *The American Journal of Physical Anthropology*. No. 94, 1994.

Snake, Doktor. *Doktor Snake's Voo Doo Spellbook*. London, UK: Eddison Sadd, 2000.

Southall, Richard. *How to be a Ghost Hunter*. St. Paul, MN: Llewellyn, 2003.

Thorsson, Edred. *Futhark: A Handbook of Rune Magic*. York Beach, ME: Samuel Weiser, 1984.

Warren, Joshua P. *How to Hunt Ghosts: A Practical Guide*. New York: Fireside, 2003.

Websites

Bookrags.com
Dictionary.com
Donoho Design Group: Ddg.com
Enter.net

Georgia Perimeter College: Gpc.edu
Hauntedplaces.com
LarryAvisBrown.homestead.com
No-Frills Home Page: Peripatus.gen.nz
Paranormalghost.com
Professorshouse.com

Psychic-revalation.com
Soul Center Therapy.com
Sunnyway.com
University of California, Museum of Paleontology: Ucmp.berkeley.edu
Wirenot.net